The
DRAMA
of the
RESURRECTION

Morton Kelsey

The
DRAMA
of the
RESURRECTION

Transforming Christianity

New City Press

Dedicated to my great-grandson
Alexander Eric Johnson

With gratitude to John Neary and Rosalind Sakata

Published in the United States by New City Press
202 Cardinal Rd., Hyde Park, NY 12538
©1999 Morton Kelsey

Cover design by Nick Cianfarani

The cover artwork is from The Apparition of Jesus to Saint Thomas, Subiaco, Italy.

Library of Congress Cataloging-in-Publication Data:

Kelsey, Morton T.
    Drama of the Resurrection / by Morton Kelsey.
    p. cm.
  Includes bibliographical references.
  ISBN 1-56548-119-4 (pbk.)
    1. Jesus Christ--Passion. 2. Jesus Christ--Resurrection. I.
Title.
  BT431 .K445 1999
  232.9'7--dc21   99-10358
                                              CIP

Printed in Canada

Contents

Introduction

The Light of God Breaks into a Dark and Evil World

One of the finest modern novelists, Reynolds Price, is also one of the finest translators of the New Testament. Price is convinced that the Gospel of John is an eyewitness account of the life of Jesus.[1] And the first paragraph of John's Gospel points to the dramatic nature of the life of Jesus, the Messiah, that is about to unfold before the reader's eyes: "In the beginning there was the spirit which created all things. What has come into being in him was life, and the light was the light of all people. The light shines in the darkness and the darkness did not overcome it" (Jn 1:4-5).[2]

However, the darkness tried to put out the light, tried to extinguish it. The conflict between the darkness and the light is the incredible drama of the resurrection. In this conflict, life and love and hope were not extinguished, but it took a crucifixion and Jesus rising from the grave before the light was established in this darkened world. The best of human beings was murdered before the drama was complete. This story demonstrates that no drama is finished until the curtain falls on the last scene. No one would have expected what occurred in this last part of Jesus' life; the drama looked like utter tragedy until the last scene.

The resurrection of Jesus from the dead nearly two thousand years ago is the most important and hopeful event in human and cosmic history. It occurred during the reign of the Emperor Tiberius Caesar. At that time Rome ruled the entire Mediterranean world with an iron hand; Rome's armies of trained and efficient killers had conquered city after city and province after province. Those who would not submit to Rome were either enslaved (three-fifths of the Empire were slaves) or they were tortured and killed, usually nailed to crosses and left to hang there naked until they died. This was the death decreed for Jesus of Nazareth by the Roman governor, Pontius Pilate. Sometimes hundreds were crucified at a time. In Jesus' case, two other men were crucified with him, and the three died together.

There is no way to understand the resurrection without facing the brutal cruelty of crucifixion. Few of us would have the courage to witness an actual crucifixion and see the depth of human evil it portrays. But it does not take much imagination to picture this brutality; I have described what Jesus of Nazareth endured in a little book, *The Cross*. The families and friends of crucifixion victims usually remained with their executed loved ones until the soldiers broke their legs to hasten their death or until they died "naturally" of asphyxiation. Where Jesus underwent this torment, a secret follower of his was watching, a wealthy man named Joseph who had a tomb nearby. He gave it to Jesus' family and stood with them until Jesus drew his last breath. Joseph and the men of Jesus' family took the body down from the cross and laid it across the knees of Mary, the mother of Jesus. Others brought a shroud. They wrapped the linen cloth around the body, and a small cortege carried Jesus' body up to the tomb and rolled a huge stone in front of it. There was nothing else to do except weep. It was dark outside and within. The women scurried around to find spices with which to embalm Jesus' body. The men retreated to their hide-out; they were in terror for fear the soldiers and officials might seek them and arrest them as co-conspirators and hang them on the crosses which always stood there as a warning to subject people.

The next thirty-six hours are beyond my ability to describe. I myself have felt that utter hopelessness, when every breath was agony. Most of us have. Most of us have known total agony and inner pain, pain far worse than any physical pain. In this case, the women were more fortunate than the men; at least they had something to do.

Jesus was the best and most holy person his followers had ever known. He knew the secret depth of life, and he taught his followers about the kingdom of God. It became more real to them than any physical kingdom.

They had set their entire hope on Jesus; he would bring the new era, the New Kingdom.

They had lived with Jesus' vision for three years. With their own eyes they had seen cripples walk as he touched them. They had seen the blind see, even those born blind. They had seen Jesus raise the dead. He had talked to the wind and it had calmed; he had healed demoniacs. This man was life and light, and now he was dead, murdered. God was dead. Both the men and the women broke out in compulsive weeping. Everything that they had believed in and had hoped for was swept away by a mighty darkness. All that was left was a vast and barren desert, and in this desert they were stranded.

They gave up all hope. They could hardly move. They thought to themselves: "What is the use of going on? Everything is meaningless." One of them gave up totally: Judas, who had betrayed Jesus. And Jesus would have received and healed him, too, if he had not hanged himself; Robert Buchanan suggests this in his poem "The Ballad of Jesus Iscariot."[3]

For three days the followers of Jesus lost all hope. The Son of God, the Light of God, the Messiah was destroyed. God was dead or did not care.

But as we shall see, this was not the end. In spite of or because of the crucifixion on Good Friday, Jesus rose from the dead. He brought hope to his mother and to his disciples, and he founded the most glorious and hopeful religion and festival the world has ever known. The opening words of the Gospel of John are true. The true light which created the world appeared in the darkness, and the darkness did not overcome it. We do not know where the darkness came from, but it did not quench the light. Instead it created the drama of resurrection, the most glorious human festival. Only heaven may provide a more magnificent festival than Eastertide.

The Darkness Attacks

When Jesus was born, evil was already trying to keep the Son of God from surviving in this dark world. Herod's soldiers tried to find Jesus and murder him, but Joseph listened to the voice of the angel, God's messenger. At the angel's urging, the holy family fled to Egypt. Only after Herod was dead did Joseph take his family to Nazareth. There Jesus attended the synagogue and studied the Old Testament. He also learned his father's trade and was an excellent carpenter. When his father died, Jesus supported his family.

And then he heard his call. John was baptizing in the Jordan River, and Jesus went down to be baptized by John. As Jesus emerged from the water, he heard a voice saying, "This is my beloved son in whom I am well pleased." Looking up to heaven, he "saw the spirit as a dove descending on him." He knew that he must find his calling (Lk 3:13-17).

He left John and fled into the wild Judean desert mountains. There he fasted for forty days and forty nights, and at the end he was hungry. Then the drama of Christianity began. The evil one, the dark[4] one, appeared to tempt him and to turn him away from his mission. Jesus, because of his fasting, was very hungry; he knew the hungry fellowship of the human race. The evil one said to him, "If you are the Son of God, turn the stones into loaves of bread and then you can feed yourself and be the great benefactor of humanity." But this temptation did not deceive Jesus who replied, "One does not live by bread alone, but by every word that comes from the mouth of God" (Mt 4:12-17).

Then the devil took him to the holy city, placed him at the top of a tall pinnacle, and said to him, "If you are the Son of God, throw yourself off and the angels will bear you up so you do not dash your foot against a stone." But Jesus knew that his mission was not to make a display of meaningless miraculous powers, and he replied, "Away with you, Satan, for it is written: 'Do not put the Lord your God to the test.'"

Then the devil took Jesus to the top of a very high mountain, showed him all the kingdoms of the world and their splendor, and said to him, "All these will I give to you if you will fall down and worship me." Jesus said to him, "Away with you, Satan, for it is written: worship the Lord your God and serve only him." The devil's promises were not empty; the dark one really has all this to give. When we want the kind of power the devil offered Jesus, we have fallen into the clutches of darkness.

Then the evil one, who had surrounded Jesus like a dark cloud, disappeared, and angels came and ministered to Jesus.

Satan realized that a frontal attack on the Son of God would bear no fruit; he realized he could not corrupt Jesus. He would have to corrupt mortals, who would then destroy the light of the Son of God, for evil cannot tolerate holiness and goodness defeating its plans.

As I have said, there is no more hopeful festival in any religion than the feast of the resurrection. It assures us that there is meaning and hope in our world—light in our darkness, joy and beauty in the heart of God who made us. Why is it, then, that so few people are willing to contemplate the events of the resurrection? First of all, before contemplating the resurrection we have to look at the crucifixion and see and feel the pain of evil and darkness that is woven throughout our world. The crucifixion makes resurrection necessary, or life is meaningless; resurrection, therefore, forces us to look at the worst in life in order to have the incredibly magnificent joy of heaven. In addition, since the descriptions of the resurrection events are scattered throughout the New Testament, we must know the Bible well. We must study scripture closely if we are to see and know and feel the full resurrection history. Sadly, even during my seminary training no one suggested that I study all the accounts and aspects of the resurrection to see the consistent picture that emerges.

During the blitz in World War II, as the bombs were raining down on England, all the churches—Catholic, Anglican, and nonconformist—realized that the people needed moral support. So they commissioned Dorothy Sayers to write and produce twelve radio plays describing the life of Christ. People all over Britain huddled around their wirelesses waiting for the next episode. I read these radio plays in the book *The Man Born to Be King* while traveling to Texas for an Easter conference. I found in these plays the account of the resurrection that I had been looking for and needed. Here was an account of the events that transformed the utter defeat of Good Friday into a smashing victory in which the defeat of light was transformed into the victory for light, and the Roman Empire became the base from which Christianity spread out over the whole world. I will follow the basic outline of Dorothy Sayers' brilliant radio plays, in which she shows how the defeat of Good Friday became the victory of the resurrection.

Chapter 1

The Tragedy of Judas

In order to appreciate the depth and power of Jesus' resurrection let us step back again into the lives of his friends and followers, who experienced deep desolation after Jesus had suffered and died. Let us enter into their agony and then watch their transformation as they confront the empty tomb and the appearances of Jesus to them.

Saturday, the Sabbath, was nearly as unbearable as Friday, the day of crucifixion. The shock of Friday began to wear off, and now Jesus' followers experienced fully their utter despair and grief. The person whom they loved was dead; they had watched him suffer and die. The sword pierced through his mother's heart and through the hearts of his friends and disciples. Jesus' excruciating death destroyed the one they loved and their very reason for living. Their religious foundations crumbled and were washed away in a river of tears. Jesus had spoken of a God of love, a divine Lover; but if such a God existed, apparently this God did not intervene in the world. Doubts clawed their way into their hearts and minds. Could Jesus have been wrong? Was he deceived? Were they wrong to have given up their ordinary lives to follow him?

Agony swept over the disciples on the Sabbath when they could do no work. They were like criminals in solitary confinement, with nothing to think about but the horror of their meaningless lives. The disciples huddled together in a rented house, each knock at the door bringing terror. They imagined that they heard the sound of marching feet, soldiers, the temple guard; they imagined more crosses stark against the sky. The emotional state of the women was a bit better. They made plans for his embalming, for securing the spices, the myrrh and labdanum. (Funeral preparations can have a psychological value.) Friday night none of the followers slept; the pain was intolerable. But on the Sabbath night their bodies were kinder, and they slept in spite of their torment.

Judas' reaction was quite different from the grief of the other apostles. He went out and hanged himself. Poor Judas—he was such a complicated mixture of conflicting motives and emotions. His action was a natural reaction to the hopeless darkness that devoured him. A fine portrayal of this tragic character is found in Dorothy Sayers' *The Man Born to Be King*.[1] Who was this man, Judas, whom Jesus selected for his gifts and potential and who, like Satan (one of God's finest creations), went wrong and brought tragedy and mayhem into the world? The powers of evil had their day; they possessed and defeated Judas, even though they were defeated in the process.

Judas may have been a disciple of John the Baptist invited to join Jesus' band of followers at the time of John's imprisonment. He was able, brilliant, enthusiastic. He handled the treasury for the little fellowship. Whether he sought out the religious leaders who wished to get rid of Jesus or whether they sought him out, we will never know. But somehow Judas and Caiaphas came together, and Judas was given thirty pieces of silver—the price for the freeing of a slave—to betray his master. The night before Jesus' death, Judas left their Last Supper together and went out to the temple precincts. From there he led the band selected to seize Jesus and bring him in for trial. They had chosen to seize Jesus at night, for Jesus' many followers among the common people would be safely in bed and thus would not be aroused. Judas led the temple guard to Jesus' secret rendezvous in the Garden of Gethsemane, and he went up to Jesus and kissed him.

Jesus knew this was the sign for the temple guards to seize him. But Jesus asked Judas, "Friend, would you betray the Son of Man with a kiss?" Even in extremity, he treated his betraying disciple as a prodigal son.

What were Judas' motives? Like yours and mine, they were mixed. Part of him had come to believe that Jesus might be an impostor, a fraud, that Jesus appeared to be someone he was not. Another part felt that Jesus was not stepping into his messiahship as he should and that Judas' act might force Jesus into action.

Still another fragment of his being (of which he may not even have been conscious) was angry because Peter, not he, was called the Rock. Still another contributing factor was his inability to say no when he met with Caiaphas; his hand itched for the money. Judas loved and hated Jesus at the same time. But he probably never thought that his action would lead to Jesus' crucifixion. Unfortunately, human emotions are not logical and can be totally ambivalent. Often we, too much like Judas, betray those closest to us through no clearly conscious motive, carried along by the forces of the unconscious of which we are not aware. Someone has suggested that the essence of sin may lie in unconsciousness, which opens us to evil as well as good, and sweeps us along without our knowing where we are moving or why.

Judas watched from afar and saw the faithful disciples take down the dead bodies from their crosses. All night he tossed and turned, more and more aware of the evil he had done. He could find no defense for himself; and since Jesus' message of God's unfathomable love had not reached his deepest being, his despair grew deeper and deeper. In the morning he tried to return the money to the temple officials, and they laughed at him.

He could imagine no resolution to his situation. How could he ever face those intimate friends of three days before? They might even kill him. The black mood, the hopelessness, became intolerable. Then Judas betrayed himself; he went out and hanged himself. When the disciples gathered together to select a successor to Judas, Peter told an even more bitter account of Judas' death than we find in Matthew's Gospel (Mt 27:3-9; Acts 1:15-20). The tragic irony of Judas' death was that if he had borne his despair one day longer, Jesus might well have come to him and transformed him, just as after the resurrection he came with new life to others who had abandoned and denied him.

Chapter 2

The Empty Tomb

On Sunday, the first day of the week, just as the sun was rising and dawn gave them enough light to find their way, Mary of Magdala, Mary the mother of Jesus, and Salome gathered up the embalming spices they had purchased the night before when the Sabbath ended at sunset. They set out for Jesus' tomb to prepare the body for burial. As they walked along they were talking with one another, heartbroken, discussing how they could remove the great stone that closed the tomb. As the tomb came into sight they saw that the stone had already been rolled away. They wondered who had tampered with the tomb. Had someone broken in to desecrate their master's body and resting place? As they shared these fears they broke into a run and dashed the last hundred yards right into the tomb. They quickly saw that the body they had placed there was gone; the tomb was empty.

As their eyes adjusted to the shadowy light of the
tomb, they were amazed, astonished, frightened. In the
place where they had tenderly laid Jesus' body, an unearthly being was sitting—a young man wearing a shining white robe. The angel saw how frightened the
women were, and he hastened to reassure them that he
was a messenger of God and brought the best possible
news. The women were stunned; it is an awesome experience to come face to face with the holy, the messenger
of God or the essence of the divine. Throughout the Bible, in the Old Testament and the New, angelic beings
apologize for their overwhelming power and the fear
they inspire. And today the divine still touches us, and
still strikes us with awe. Our hymns still sing of angels,
whom I call "tentacles of divine brilliance."[1]

The angel spoke directly to the women: "Do not be
afraid. You are looking for Jesus of Nazareth who was
crucified. Look, here is the place where they laid him.
He is risen. He is not here. Go now and give this message to his disciples and Peter: 'He will go on before you
into Galilee, and you will see him there, just as he told
you.'"

These words frightened the women even more than
the dazzling presence of the holy being. The angel's
news was overwhelming, and the women could not
comprehend what they had encountered. They fled out
of the tomb, beside themselves with amazement and
awe. They ran away and at first said nothing to anyone,
for they were terrified. (We should remember that the
testimony of women was doubted in Jewish courts, and
the disciples had not yet encountered the risen Christ.)

What an incredibly powerful experience these follow-ers of Jesus had. And one of the most convincing parts of the resurrection narrative is the simple way it is pre-sented. It is no wonder that the women did not go and tell their experience to the other disciples immediately; they knew their account would not be accepted as real-ity. And when they did tell their story, the apostles did not believe them. But one by one Jesus appeared to his followers, and transformation took place in each of them.

I had read the account of the empty tomb dozens and dozens of times before I perceived what was actu-ally written. The women at the empty tomb panicked and ran away. Only when we are touched by similar fears can we appreciate the depth and power of the res-urrection. *Had most of us been making up this story we would have written it quite differently.* We would have probably concluded it something like this: "And when the women saw the shining divine messenger sitting in the tomb, they were astonished. But the holy being spoke to them, telling them that Jesus had risen from the dead and that they were to go and tell the disciples and then go to Galilee to meet him. At these words the women wept for joy and threw their arms around each other. For a few moments they were silent, and then the joy-ous cry broke forth from their lips: 'He is risen, He is risen. The Lord is risen indeed.' Then they dashed forth from the tomb with light steps and ran down the hill-side calling out to everyone they met. 'He is risen. He is risen indeed, alleluia.' They found the other disciples, and they all rejoiced at the good news the women brought; soon afterward all of them set off for Galilee."

But this is not the way the gospel tells it. The women were terrified and ran off, telling no one because they were afraid. And they had reason to be afraid. Remember what they had been through—the seizure of Jesus in the garden, the trial before the Sanhedrin, sentencing before Pilate, the hours of watching Jesus die on the cross, the derision of the crowd, sleepless nights and dark, hopeless days. Then they met the dazzling holiness in the tomb. The women had given up any hope as they took the broken body from the cross. They had not been present when Jesus predicted his passion and rising from the dead, and we can be sure that the disciples did not understand Jesus well enough to share such dark forebodings.

They needed Jesus' humanness to soften the fearful intensity of his holiness. They would understand this later, but now they were simply overwhelmed. They were torn between doubt and fear. If the angel's words were true, and that bright immensity that encountered them could not be denied, then they had built their lives on all the wrong assumptions. Suddenly they were confronted with a world in which God was more powerful than Rome or any power. And what is more, God cared what was going on among human beings and *did something about it.*

Of course, a part of them rejoiced in the hope that Jesus had risen, but primarily they were stupefied and paralyzed with fear, and they did not know what to believe. Perhaps the world *was* the way Jesus had described it. But they had never quite believed him. It is all well and good to talk about spiritual things and spiritual powers, to carry on long and involved discussions about spiritual reality, but it is another matter to find ourselves in the hand of the living God who has made heaven and earth, who has stretched out the stars and fashioned the uncanny intricacy of subatomic particles. To find that this one cares about us and is watching with us sends chills down our spines and shocks of amazement through our hearts.

A person's initial reaction to such an experience is likely to be fear. The resurrection was not a sentimental Easter card, but a profound revolution and revelation, an awe-filled one. The incredible love of God in the risen Jesus assumes its deepest significance as it springs out of our fear and amazement. Those of us who have met this risen Jesus in deep despair and have been raised out of it really know the meaning of the resurrection; Jesus' love, however, still amazes us.

Many people turn away from the resurrection because of its frightening aspect. They would prefer to have life knowable and tame and ordered, at least partially within their control. If the resurrection is true, then this world is not what it seems, and I may be called upon to follow the way of love revealed in this event. Love may demand all of me, and this will require courage—the kind of courage that the first disciples of Jesus showed as they went out singing the good news in a hostile and persecuting empire.

Peter and John

Mary Magdalene did not enter the tomb with the other women. Her only thought was that someone had stolen the body away, and in utter despair she dropped her bundles of spices and ran off to find Peter. She found Peter and John together and blurted out that the tomb was open and someone had stolen the body from the tomb; she had no idea where they had placed it. Peter and John set right off toward the tomb. They were running side by side, but John was younger and faster and reached the tomb before Peter. He looked in and saw the strange orderliness of the grave wrappings lying quite undisturbed, as if the body of Jesus had evaporated, leaving the grave clothes lying there. He was also struck by the electrifying numinous quality within the tomb, and he hesitated to enter it. He thought that this was more than it seemed. He saw and believed that Jesus had risen from the dead. He knew.

Impulsive Peter came up moments later and rushed headlong into the tomb. He, too, noted the order which reigned there. Whatever else, this was not the work of grave robbers. He examined the carefully folded linen shroud and the cloth that was rolled up just as it had been around Jesus' head. Peter was struck by what he saw and also by something more than his eyes were seeing. Jesus' intimations about dying and rising on the third day came back to him. So Peter saw and wanted to believe. Perhaps he sensed the presence of the risen Jesus.

Peter felt hope rise within his heart—and yet part of him remained afraid that this hope was vain. He and John looked at each other. The look said, "We must go and tell the others what we have discovered." Both of them were wrapped deep in thought as they emerged from the tomb and started back to find the others. John was expectant and at peace; Peter was torn between doubt and hope. They forgot all about Mary, who lingered near the tomb weeping.

One thing was sure. Finding the tomb empty was not enough. It was necessary, because without the empty tomb Jesus' appearances would simply be like other appearances of deceased people at the times of their deaths or later. These are comforting and helpful experiences and in a sense show that death is not final, but they tell us nothing about conquering death in this world, in the here and now. The resurrection of Jesus, in other words, was far more than just an appearance of a deceased person after death while the body lies in the funeral home. The resurrection of Jesus was both *spiritual and physical.* The physical body was transformed into something far more glorious. The worlds of the physical and spiritual met and joined. Creation was totally complete. The darkness was defeated.

Had there been only the empty tomb with its neatly laid-out grave clothes and angels, only the spiritually attuned people like John would believe. But God knew that we human beings need more than authority and logic if we are going to believe that Love is real, powerful, death-conquering. God knew that we human beings need to have experiences of the risen Jesus. To *be*

convinced means *to be conquered by*, and without the convincing and overpowering experiences of the risen Jesus, the victorious Christ, there would have been a less
courageous Christian Church to pit itself against the
Roman Empire. In only three centuries the Christians
conquered that Empire in spite of persecution, torture,
and ridicule. Without the resurrection, Jesus' followers
would not have believed that their master was indeed
the incarnation of God and worth dying for. This is a
matter of *both/and* and not *either/or*. *Both* empty tomb
and meetings with the physically risen Jesus were necessary for a victorious Christianity. The early Church
knew this well when it fought against the belief that
God only *appeared* to be incarnate and only *seemed* to die
on the cross. The coming of God in the flesh and the
resurrection told the disciples (and tells us) that this
physical world is God's world and that divine Love has
ultimate power in both. It speaks to the ultimate unity
of the world in which we live. I feel sorry for small-
minded Christians who do not see the wild mystery of
God's world—a world of quantum mechanics and small
particle physics,[2] a world in which resurrection must
and does occur, a world where love is ultimately su-
preme.

Chapter 3

Mary of Magdala

Mary of Magdala was in no condition to make infer-
ences about a risen Jesus. She needed him, and he came
to her. His appearance to her touched and transformed
Mary. After finding Peter and John, she walked back
aimlessly toward the sepulchre. From a distance and in
deep thought she saw them enter and then come out.
They did not notice Mary, and they walked away toward Jerusalem by another way. Mary cried all the way
back to the grave, and she stood beside the entrance
weeping as if her eyes were a bottomless well of tears.

Mary had been lost. Most people looking at her
would have shaken their heads and said that there was
no point trying to help her. Luke—who may have
known her well—wrote that she was the one from
whom Jesus had cast out seven devils. Whatever else
"to be possessed and delivered from seven devils"
means, it means that she had been sick in body, soul,

and mind. She had fallen into utter depravity. She was morally lost, and the lostness of her soul led her into such anguish of mind that she became mentally sick. The sickness of her mind wracked her body, and she was tormented and ill. Mary was broken, poor in spirit, worthless. And Jesus healed her.

Tradition identifies her with the brazen woman who broke into the dinner party for men given by Simon the Pharisee, something no decent woman would have done. She went behind Jesus as he reclined to eat, broke open an alabaster vase, and poured the precious ointment out on him; she washed his feet with her tears and wiped them with her hair. Mary had fallen in every way, and she had considered herself as hopeless as others considered her. She had indeed been tormented by seven spirits of weakness and sin, but Jesus had cast them out and Mary was whole again. No wonder she burst in upon that party. She had to let him know she was well. The host watched, shocked that this man would let such a woman touch him. Jesus read his thoughts and told a story about forgiveness, and then he spoke a new truth: Those who are forgiven the most are the most blessed—this is the mystery of human brokenness and failure. Jesus paid Mary the highest compliment he paid to anyone in the gospel narrative of this encounter.

Her tears continued to flow as Mary went back to the tomb. She was thinking to herself: "He saved me and I thought I had found meaning, hope, and life. I believed that he was God incarnate. He was like God to me. But once again I was a fool; it was all illusion, all a sham. I was deceived again, but this time by a noble person. I saw in him more than was actually there; he was just a noble man. The world and its hurting people can't stand nobility—they destroy it. They destroyed him, and they have destroyed me too. Still I will go back to the tomb and see if I can find his body and do what I can."

Mary was confused and desperate. When we can identify with what she was going through, then we can understand Mary's actions. What a comfort it is for me in my darkness and most helpless moments, when everything has caved in on me and I see no hope, to accompany Mary to that empty tomb in my heart in contemplation. I can stoop down with her and look into the tomb. She did not find his body there. She did not even see the grave clothes. Instead, she saw two majestic shining white figures—one seated where Jesus' head had been, another seated at the foot of the slab. Ordinarily such numinous figures would have sent chills of terror through her, but Mary was too full of grief to be shaken by the strange quality of these figures. She could not have been more frightened or despairing; indeed, if they had destroyed her at that moment, it would have only been relief. One of them broke the silence with these words: "Woman, why are you weeping?"

At this a fresh flood of tears poured from Mary's eyes. She caught her breath and explained, "They have taken my Lord's body and I do not know where they put him." It is bad enough to lose the one you loved. It is worse to see life crash in because everything that the dead one stood for appears to have been unreal. But now they had stolen his body; the only thing left to touch had been snatched away. Mary needed to anoint the broken body of her friend and master; this service for the dead might have eased the pain and brought closure to her grief. But the theft of his body was the final desecration. Not being able to perform the last ritual was the end of the road, the last indignity, a final stab at her heart. No wonder she wept. Her eyes were so blurred with tears that she was not sure what she saw inside the tomb. Mary had held herself together during the actual nailing of Jesus to the cross and the hours that he hung there. She had helped take down his body and carry it to the tomb. But now that she found his body gone, she was hysterical with pain and anguish.

She did not know what to make of those creatures in the tomb. What a silly and ironic question they asked about her weeping. She stood up and turned around and nearly bumped into a man standing behind her. He was wearing peasant clothes, and she thought he must be a gardener who had come early after the Sabbath to tend the garden. He also spoke to her: "Woman, why are you crying? Who is it that you are looking for?" They seemed like matter-of-fact questions at the time; only later did the memory of them reveal to her the touch of divine irony. For several minutes her only answer was another deluge of tears. At length she controlled herself enough to speak. In a pleading voice she said, "If you took him away, sir, tell me where you have put him and I will go and get him." She was looking right at Jesus, but she was separated from him by a veil of tears and unbelief. She turned away in hopelessness when he did not answer her.

And then he spoke one simple word: "Mary." He called her by her own name. Then she recognized his voice. Jesus had spoken that name with warmth and care when others spoke it only with scorn and derision. It was his voice that had first broken through the wall around her heart. She had determined that no one would ever enter that heart again, but this voice had knocked so quietly that she had let him in. Then came the agony of coming back to life, like stepping on a leg that had gone to sleep. Now he spoke her name again, and this time the voice brought only joy and peace. Mary's tears dried up, and a smile of unearthly joy lit up her entire face—she went from darkest night to sunny noonday in one moment.

I need to listen again and again to the way that Mary cried out "Rabboni!" Each syllable had a new quality. It was like a bird song. She had always called him Rabboni or Teacher, but this time the word had new depth and meaning. She wiped the rest of the tears from her face with one quick gesture and stretched out her arms to embrace his ankles. The body that she had come to anoint for burial was standing there before her, radiant in health, glowing like the rays of the rising sun just now beginning to bathe the garden in light.

Then Jesus spoke softly to her: "Not yet, Mary. Cease holding on to me, because I have not yet gone back up to my Father. But go to my brothers and sisters and tell them for me what you have experienced, and tell them that I go back to my Father and your Father,

to my God and your God." Mary needed to cease cling-
ing to Jesus' human body, and she got the message. Jesus then vanished from her sight, but everything made
sense to Mary now. She threw back her head and sang
(Jn 20:11-18).

She danced down the hill; she was chanting, "Rabboni, Rabboni!" She knew that he was the teacher, the
master, the lord, the conqueror, God. She had been
right to let that voice break into the sealed fortress of
her heart. Meaning and love and hope were real. People
did not just use one another. The universe did not just
use people and cast them off. What a beautiful morning it was! The flowers were blooming in the garden,
primroses and wild lilies, roses, red and white; she was
as alive as they were. The world was green and new. She
picked flowers and tossed them into the air.

She found the disciples huddled together with some
friends, and she told them: "I have seen the Lord."
They smiled indulgent smiles, thinking to themselves
that pain works in strange ways on some minds. They
were courteous; they did not tell her that she was
dreaming or crazy. But this doubt didn't bother Mary
because she knew, really knew. She had knelt on the
ground and clutched his legs and was told to let go. She
knew that he was alive. There was nothing left to fear,
not even death or grief or pain or anything. When Jesus
came to them later, it was Mary's turn to smile.

The same kind of transforming experience continued
on through the apostolic age and then down through
the centuries and still happens today. The gift of the
Holy Spirit means many things, but one very impor-

tant activity of the Spirit is to bring us experiences of this rescuing and saving risen Christ.

Mary's experience of the risen Jesus gives an enlarged picture of the deepest and most powerful kind of religious experience. Jesus has appeared to many over the centuries. I wrote an introduction to a book of such experiences, *I Am with You Always*. It tells of many such experiences that were told to a religious psychologist.[1]

Chapter 4

Jesus Comes to Peter

The refusal to see eternal meaning for the human soul in spite of all the evidence to the contrary may well be a cop-out, a fear of having to take eternal responsibility for ourselves. Most people who have experienced near encounters with death and *know* that they did not cease to be are quite careful about whom they tell their experiences to. People are shaken by their accounts.

With the resurrection of Jesus in mind, let us listen to the experiences that the other disciples had with their Risen Lord. Once we are potentially open to these mysterious encounters, we will find one or two of these meetings that are particularly meaningful to us. In addition, the total account has an impact that one account cannot have. Paul, in his First Letter to the Corinthians, wrote these words: "First and foremost, I handed on to you the facts which had been imparted to me: that Christ died for our sins, in accordance with the scriptures; that he was buried; that he was raised to life on the third day, according to the scriptures; and that he appeared to Cephas, and afterwards to the Twelve. Then he appeared to over five hundred of our brothers at once, most of whom are still alive, although some have died. Then he appeared to James, and afterwards to all the apostles" (1 Cor 15:5-9). Paul then goes on to say that Jesus even appeared to him, although he had been monstrous in persecuting the Church.

Paul's letter is the earliest written account of the resurrection; it reports an early appearance of Jesus to Peter, whom Jesus called Cephas, which is not recorded in the four gospels. Like the resurrection, this appearance was probably so basic to the spoken gospel message that it was not thought necessary to write about it in detail. Without this experience, how could Peter have preached with authority? To appreciate the significance of Jesus' encounter with Peter, we need to put ourselves in Peter's shoes as he heard the cock crow the second time during Jesus' trial.

When the cock crowed the second time, anguish struck Peter like a knife between his ribs; he had just denied Jesus for the third time. Peter walked a little way apart and wept bitterly, tears flooding over his weather-beaten, wrinkled cheeks. No wonder he wept—he had denied his master. It happened just as Jesus had predicted. All Peter's professions of loyalty flooded back into his mind: "Oh, no, master, I will never leave you. Even if I have to die with you I will not leave you." The tears welled up from the very center of his being, from the bottom of his heart. Was there anything to staunch this flood? Could anything heal the breach in his inner being made by his denials? Would he ever be able to hold his head high again? Weeping and broken, Peter wandered off into the night to find those who had not even had the courage to follow Jesus to trial. They, too, had made bold vows of loyalty.

Very often we feel like Peter—we realize we have denied the risen Jesus in our speech and actions. Often when confronted with all of ourselves we feel like Peter and wonder if there is any hope for us. One of the reasons we spend so little time in silence is that when we stop and listen to our inner depths we are faced with our betrayals and unconsciousness. If we can stay busy enough, we can often avoid facing the many ways we have betrayed our own souls, our God, the Holy Spirit, Jesus, what we know is right and holy and good. We have seen the noblest people around us go down in defeat, mocked and derided, and we stood by denying or saying nothing. But we suddenly remember what we thought we stood for, and then come the tears and the despair. We are so much like Peter.

Peter remembered the supper at which he had spoken so boldly and his failure to stay awake when Jesus had pleaded with him to give human support. Jesus, in agony, wrestled through the decision of whether he would stay and suffer crucifixion or flee and save his life. The soldiers came, and Judas gave his master the kiss of death. For a few moments the apostles were brave: as long as they had swords in their hands. At Jesus' command, however, they put away their swords, and then they fled.

Peter followed the band of soldiers at a distance to the house of Caiaphas and waited in the courtyard outside. A servant girl saw him warming himself over a brazier and said to him: "You were with this man from Nazareth, Jesus." Peter denied it. Peter might have admitted to the soldiers or to the high priest that he was a follower, but not to this servant. (So it is with us. We deny Jesus in little things, to insignificant people, where it does not seem to matter.) The servant asked Peter a second time, and again he denied that he knew him. And then a bystander who heard him speak remarked: "You must be one of them, for your accent is that of a Galilean." And this time Peter cried out with an oath: "I do not know this man you speak of." Then the cock crowed, and Peter burst into tears. Imagine how Peter felt—three times he had said that he did not know Jesus.

Peter fled. He found some of the other disciples hiding in a locked room like dumb and broken animals. Peter was so distraught that he could hardly speak. He did not have the courage to follow Jesus before Pilate or wait at the foot of the cross. He wondered if Jesus really would have wanted him there. Peter knew he had failed. The Twelve had failed, except for the Beloved Disciple.

Could anything make a man of Peter again? What could ever restore his self-respect? What could give him some peace again, some hope for himself? No human action could mend the wound of Peter's denial—no amount of human caring or comfort, counseling or psychiatry. Nothing that Peter did or could do would be able to restore him and make him feel like a decent human being once again. As he waited those dark days, Peter doubted that he could ever stop loathing himself. And yet Peter became a courageous man, a saint, one of the foundation stones of the Christian fellowship that conquered the ancient world. How did it all happen?

Jesus rose from the dead and naturally sought Peter out. No one more than Peter needed forgiveness to make him a disciple again. And what a disciple he became. Jesus came to Peter radiant with life and wholeness. We do not know the details of this encounter; but we know that in that meeting with the risen Jesus of Nazareth, Peter was transformed. He was reborn and able to start all over again. The past was wiped away. Peter was accepted, forgiven, and given a fresh start. His encounter with the loving, risen Jesus told Peter that this is a world of second chances. Jesus' rising from death took away the finality of Peter's denial and failure.

When Peter preached the good news he would say: "If Jesus cared enough for me who denied him to come to me, does he not care for you? Will he not come to you in your need?" Neither our denials nor Peter's can destroy the Spirit; such denials cannot separate us from the risen Christ. He is stronger than our weakness. The resurrection told Peter and those of us like him that we need not despair; the resurrection lifts the burden of ourselves from ourselves.

Jesus sought out Mary and he sought out Peter. The risen Jesus, like the purely human Jesus, loved Peter and came to him and expressed that love. It was not just the implications of resurrection that were important to Peter; the concrete details also mattered. Peter's master still cared, loved, forgave, and sought him out, not in spite of his weaknesses and failures but even because of them, because Peter needed him so much. And those who are forgiven the most love the most. The risen Jesus seeks us out in the very same way and stands at the door of our souls knocking and asking to be let in. We can let him in as we receive his body and blood in the eucharist, as we stop in silence to open the door to contemplate his knocking, or as we call out in despair for his saving power.

Tradition tells me that Peter stands at the gateway of heaven to let us in. What an unexpected and delightful joy to find Peter there with the keys to the kingdom around his waist. Christianity is the *only* religion that offers free forgiveness of sins to those who ask; it has built this idea into its very creeds. Peter at the gate of heaven reminds us that when I come to that place I will not be asked about all my failures and mistakes; rather, I will only be asked if I will allow the love portrayed in Jesus' resurrection from death on a cross to touch me and transform me. The power of the resurrection was for Peter an incredible experience of forgiveness, and the same transforming presence is available to us today.

Why is there no clear account of Jesus' resurrection in Mark, the earliest gospel? This account shows the importance of the empty tomb as a part of the full resurrection narrative. Mark also wanted to show how the one who denied Jesus could become a cornerstone in the Christian fellowship. None of the other evangelists dared describe how Peter had failed and then been re-deemed. Christianity is a religion of forgiveness, as the lives of Augustine and many other saints demonstrate.

Chapter 5

The Stranger on the Road

Jesus had many followers who had come to Jerusalem to see him at the Passover. Now it was the first day of the week, a glorious spring day, but that only made the pain worse for Cleopas and Simon. Their lives had fallen apart—Jesus was dead. They were going home defeated, broken human beings. How different it had been five days before when they went up to Jerusalem to celebrate the Passover with Jesus. Both of them had been convinced that the time had arrived for Jesus to establish his kingdom.

They didn't know how it would happen, but some marvel would take place. The Romans would flee in terror, thrown out. The temple would be purified and the kingdom of God would be ushered in. They had arranged their affairs so that they could drop everything and follow Jesus wherever he might lead, no matter what happened. If this was not the time, they felt that it would come soon. They would stay with him until he was ready to usher in the new age.

Both of these men had often been with Jesus and his friends. He had healed Simon's brother[1] and Cleopas' daughter. They had never known anyone like Jesus. Before they knew him, their lives had been empty, hopeless. They worked from day to day; the extortion of tax collectors and the power of the rich kept them scratching to stay alive. It is hard to live in an occupied country: One's soul is never really one's own and one is tempted to join the underground, but that looked even more futile. People like Simon and Cleopas couldn't forget the crosses that lined the highways after any rebellion. Rome was very powerful and merciless.

But Jesus had given them a new vision of what life could be. Simon remarked one day to his friend: "He knows my faults and still he loves me. He seems to love me because I need his love so much. The more he forgives my grasping bitterness and sexual follies, the more whole my life becomes." Cleopas replied: "He is kind, warm, unafraid, loving, but he has incredible power, too. That power I do not understand. Power and love mixed together make an awesome combination. I never thought I would see such a combination. He lives in this world and beyond it at the same time. I wonder if he is an ordinary mortal. He'll bring the kingdom in a supernatural way."

Now they were discussing how wrong they had been. Jesus was dead, and he never raised a finger to fight back. They had spent Thursday night in Bethany and had come late Friday morning into Jerusalem. The day was black and wild. Just outside the city walls they saw three men hanging there on crosses. They could hardly believe their eyes: On the central cross hung their master, the king of the age to come, Jesus. They were struck dumb, stupefied, numb. They found some friends in the crowd, they pieced together the story of what had happened. They waited until the end, hoping for some miracle, but Jesus died like any other mortal person. They went back to Bethany waiting for the Sabbath to pass. Their lives were barren.

Sunday ultimately arrived; nothing was left but to muster strength to pick up the pieces and go on living a meaningless life in Emmaus. As they left the city, they went to see the disciples. They, too, actually resented the bright, balmy spring day; it was out of keeping with the sadness of the world. The darkness of the previous Friday would have been far more appropriate. They trudged on, talking about the things they had been through, wondering if there was anything else they should have done. They were halfway home when a stranger caught up with them; they were so deep in agonizing reminiscences that they did not notice him until he was walking alongside them, adjusting to their stride.

For a while all three walked along silently, and then the stranger spoke: "What on earth were you talking about so earnestly back there? It must have been something awful. Your voices were laced with pain." Cleopas and Simon stopped, raised their eyes from the road, and looked at the stranger. Then Cleopas said, "Are you the only person coming from Jerusalem who does not know what things happened there the past three days?" Shaking his head, the stranger asked them, "What things are you talking about?"

The story poured out of them, each one filling in details the other had forgotten. They were grateful for the stranger's willingness to listen to their grief and bear its burden with them. It really helped them to tell the story to another. He listened intently as they spoke: "All this happened to Jesus of Nazareth, a prophet powerful in speech and action before God and the Jewish people. Our chief priests and rulers were jealous and handed him over to be sentenced to death and crucified. But we had been hoping that he was the one to liberate Israel. What is more, this is the third day since all this happened, and this morning some women of our fellowship amazed us with a strange story. They went early to the tomb, but his body was gone and they could not find it. They also told a story that they had seen a vision of angels who told them that he was alive. Some of his disciples immediately went to the tomb and found everything there just as the women had said, but they did not see Jesus. Frankly, it is bad enough to grieve over losing everything without being fed such stories. It's better to face the awful truth that love never wins in this world or maybe even in the next. We just have to grind on until we die."

At this point the stranger broke in. He was almost rude: "How stupid and dull, how foolish you two are. How slow you are to catch the true meaning the prophets have been speaking for centuries. Did they not tell you that the Messiah, the anointed one, the future king of Israel, would have to suffer tragically before he entered into his glorious victory?" The two friends could hardly believe their ears. Then this man went on to reveal the meaning of the scriptures to them. Their hearts simply burned, hearing the way he explained things. They had only heard one other person ever talk like that before, and he was dead. This stranger had the deep understanding of scriptures that Jesus had. He told them that they had misunderstood the prophets; human beings never win through strength, but rather through weakness. The coming king would naturally have to die before he could assume power over all things. The stranger spoke of the suffering servant, of dying to rise again, of losing one's life to gain it. He showed them how this theme ran through the Bible. Still they did not make the connection; they did not recognize this wise stranger.

The remaining three miles to Emmaus simply vanished while they listened to him. The man told them that love conquers just because it dies willingly. The whole law and the prophets became luminous to Simon and Cleopas. Their spines tingled and they quivered and trembled in their inner being. When they came to a fork in the road, Cleopas and his friend turned off on the road which led to the village, but the stranger started to continue down the other road. Simon called to him: "Sir, why don't you stay here with us? My home is simple but the day is almost over. It is getting dark and we're hungry. You must be also. Come and share our supper with us." They were both embarrassed, for they had never asked the traveler his name, but he seemed happy to be invited. He nodded agreement and came with them to their home.

Simon showed his guest where to wash and then set a table for them. He went out to get several loaves of bread and set them on the table with a jug of wine and cups. They all sat down together. The stranger reached over and took the bread, acting as if he were the host. He said a blessing which they had heard before. He broke the bread and gave them each a piece.

Cleopas and Simon were looking at his hands when he broke the loaf; at the same time they both saw the print of nails in each hand. A shudder of mingled joy and fear passed through them. Their eyes traveled from the hands to the face. The man was a stranger no longer. It was Jesus, the very one they had loved so much, the one who had touched the innermost recesses of their hearts and given them hope. He looked straight into their faces, and his face portrayed joy and confidence, compassion and friendship, victory and love. Simon and Cleopas cried out with joy and reached out to him in amazement and bewilderment, but he vanished from their sight.

Like a storm in the desert, the streams of their joy were suddenly running full. In slightly different ways both of them thought they had been carried to the heart of love at the center of the universe. They felt like Dante as he reached the tenth and last circle of heaven and there experienced the consummation of life's meaning.

> Yet, as a wheel moves smoothly, free from
> jars,

My will and my desire were turned by love,
The love that moves the sun and the other
   stars.[2]

Strange, but Jesus' disappearing did not deflate their
joy. His very vanishing meant that he was always present, always there. Cleopas and Simon looked at one another. Without words they knew that they had each
experienced the resurrected Jesus himself. Finally they
both spoke together, almost in unison: "We must go
back to the others and let them know that the women
were right; they don't need to suffer any more." They
wanted to share what they now knew. Jesus had risen;
he died for a purpose and had risen to secure the greatest victory ever won. The friends left their food and ran
most of the seven miles back to Jerusalem.

Why did Jesus appear to these otherwise unknown
and unimportant followers on their way home, when
he had not as yet even appeared to most of the apostles? Why were Cleopas and Simon selected? Luke
doesn't give us the particulars, but we can make some
good guesses (Lk 24:13-35).

In the first place these two human beings had the
courage to pick themselves up and go on. They were
broken, but not defeated. Tragedy had befallen them,
but they girded their loins and started back to ordinary
life again. In my experience, people who battle on
through life in spite of difficulties are more likely to
find God (or be found by the Holy One) than those
who give up. The theologian Paul Tillich describes this
truth well in *The Courage to Be;* courage and persistence

can bring us through to an experience of ultimate reality.

In addition, Simon and Cleopas had not abandoned what they had experienced as real in Jesus. They remained true to their deepest experience. Even after Jesus' death, they didn't just dismiss the whole experience with Jesus and say to each other, "We were fools to have believed in that man. We were duped. Let's never discuss him again. Let's never bother about the ultimate things of life. Let's forget it all." Many people get disillusioned when the going gets rough, but these men cared too much. They continued to struggle through to an understanding of what had happened. They cared about life and they were not about to give up their search for hope.

Jesus sought them out because they still had open hearts and minds. They hadn't closed their minds with defeat; they were willing to risk being hurt again. They were willing to listen to the stranger who met them on the way and to allow hope to rise like a holy fire within them.

And finally, these two men wouldn't let the stranger go when he began to make some sense to them. When it appeared as if he would go on and leave them, they would not let him go. They hung on to him and entreated him to stay with them. Had they not done so, they might well have missed the most glorious experience of their lives. So many of us get a glimmer of light and then let it fade from us, but not Cleopas and Simon. The stranger accepted their hospitality, took bread and broke it, and their eyes were opened.

Jesus, the Christ, still appears to human beings who are open to him, although not often with the startling power with which he appeared to these two.

G. K. Chesterton tells a similar story about Francis of Assisi, who was terrified of leprosy. One day while he was traveling, he saw before him in his path a man white with the dread disease. At first Francis drew back in horror, but he got hold of himself and ran and embraced the leper and then passed on. A moment later Francis looked back and there was no one there. Francis never doubted that it was the Christ himself whom he had encountered there.[3] In a later chapter I will give several examples of how the Christ continues to come to floundering men and women and to turn their lives around.

Chapter 6

Jesus Comes to His Own

The entire Sabbath the disciples huddled together behind locked doors. The experience of the women and of John made little or no impression on them. John tried to explain to them his conviction and hope. They listened, politely shaking their heads. With typical male chauvinism, they simply dismissed Mary's account as the illusion of a simple-minded and overly emotional woman. Her very joy and peace confirmed their judgment about her mental stability. The discussions went back and forth, going nowhere. The Eleven came and went.

During the late afternoon James said, "This is all nice talk, but none of us has seen him."[1] But then Andrew—who had been out of the room—returned, strangely quiet; finally he spoke up in a low voice: "Peter has seen something." Several of them chimed in: "What's that, Andrew?"

A hush fell on the room as Peter's brother spoke: "I went to him just now, and found him stretched upon the floor. He said to me: 'The Lord is alive; I have seen him.' And I said: 'What, here?' He answered: 'Yes.' 'Well,' I said, 'what did he say to you?' Peter answered, 'Don't ask.' I laid him on his bed, and he fell instantly into a deep sleep, like a child. He is asleep now. Thomas is sitting with him."

Impatiently Philip spoke: "It was a vision, maybe, or a dream. Our Lord is dead." John replied, "Yes, Philip, I said that too, God forgive me. Yet did we not see the widow's son raised up and Lazarus called out from the grave? And what did our Lord say to you at that last Passover supper?" The conversation went on and on, but only John and Andrew spoke with any conviction. The others all wished that Jesus were alive again, but they could barely believe that it might be so. Nathanael voiced the common doubt: "You say he's alive, John. Well, what's he doing? And what are we to do? You know an order has gone out that anybody who repeats this resurrection story will be put in prison, and . . ."

It is impossible to prove the resurrection, but it is also impossible to disprove it—which is true of any fact. It is a fact that Jesus was crucified. It is a fact that his followers were transformed. The great Henri Bergson reminds us that "there is no conceivable means of establishing the impossibility of a fact."[2]

Jesus warned his disciples that even rising from the dead would not necessarily convince people that they should change their lives. In Jesus' parable, the rich man in torment in Hades pleaded with father Abraham to send someone from the dead to warn his brothers, who were as unconcerned about the poor as he had been. Abraham answered, "If they do not listen to Moses and the prophets, they will pay no heed even if someone rises from the dead." We human beings don't like to change our basic assumptions about life or reality. T. S. Kuhn notes that scientists who are forced to face facts contrary to their basic theories become very nervous and exhibit many of the symptoms of anxiety. The resurrection of Jesus overturned nearly all of the prevailing assumptions about life and reality current in his time (and, I might add, in our own). This event was an affirmation of the person who taught and lived love; it was a statement that at the heart and center of reality, in the innermost core of God, nothing exists but love.

The actual reaction of people to resurrection may well be more like that depicted by Eugene O'Neill in his drama, *Lazarus Laughed*. People in this play want nothing to do with Lazarus. He has interrupted their consuming devotion to trivial things. Mary and Martha are shocked and angry when Lazarus laughs at the news of Jesus' death. At the end of O'Neill's play the world murders Lazarus in order not to be reminded, annoyed, upset. Commenting on both the resurrection of Lazarus and the resurrection of Jesus, Paul Scherer, in his exposition of Luke in *The Interpreter's Bible*, writes these words: "The resurrection is a vista that makes our world too small. And it makes human life too great. Whenever a man comes to a huge city from the town back home, where his name was bandied about the

streets, and everybody knew his uprising and his down-
sitting, he is inclined, almost irresistibly inclined, to
scuttle in out of the limelight with a sigh of ponderous
relief! Nobody knows him, thank God! And nobody
cares what he does—thank God again! He can hide now
from a thousand responsibilities. Perhaps the doctrine
of our insignificance is a kind of wishful thinking! The
resurrection makes our dimensions too big."[3] If this
was done for us, we are far more important than we
think. There is no hiding place from Love. This is indeed frightening.

Just as the Eleven argued about the possibility of Jesus' resurrection, a loud knock shook the door. The disciples looked at one another, and Andrew spoke in
terror: "It's the end. They've come for us." They wondered what to do; one suggested that they bar the door.
Cleopas and Simon knocked again and called out,
"Don't be afraid; it is just Cleopas and Simon. We have
good news." The door was opened and then locked and
barred behind them. The whole story spilled out about
the stranger and how Jesus had revealed himself in the
breaking of the bread. Cleopas finished: "What a moment, but then in a flash he was gone. There was no one
there, but the fragments of the broken bread lay upon
the table." When several of the doubters objected that
it was just a vision, a ghost, Cleopas reminded them
that the bread *had been broken.* Increasing uneasiness
was rising among them; the stories they heard were uncanny and frightening, and the stories were multiply-
ing.

At that moment Jesus appeared there in the midst of them. He spoke his usual familiar greeting: "Peace be with you." They first looked startled, and then they shrank back terrified, almost afraid to look at him. It was as if they had been thrust into the creative dynamo in the center of the universe, into the heart of being. Numinous awe and fear struck them like a giant wave. Even Cleopas and Simon were a bit afraid as the reality of Jesus and of his glory did not fade away. The truly holy is overwhelming.

Then Jesus stretched out his scarred hands to them and said, "My friends, why are you so troubled? What are you afraid of? Why are you so overcome by doubts? Do you think that I am a ghost come to torment you? My children, it is I, your friend and master. It is I myself. Come, touch me, feel me and see that I am real, a real body. A ghost does not have flesh and bones." Still the disciples were afraid and hung back. He spoke to them again: "Do you have anything to eat?" There was something ludicrous about this numinous reality asking for food, but it broke the spell that their fear had cast upon them. They had a piece of broiled fish; they handed it to him. Right there before them he took the fish and ate it with relish. John was the first to come and touch him. Then they all began to crowd around him, touching his hands and feet. He was the same warm, human Jesus. But there was something else about him, something wonderful, yes, something uncanny but no longer frightening. They asked him questions and he answered them. He embraced each one of them tenderly. Then he explained the scriptures to them and the meaning of everything that had happened. He told them that they were to share their new vision of reality. They were to start in Jerusalem and then to go out into the Roman world and even beyond that. He also told them that he would give them the power to do all this. Several hours went by in a split second. He blessed them, and then he disappeared in just the same strange way in which he had come. A barred door made no more difference to him than the stone that had sealed the tomb.

Wild joy broke out among them. They hugged one another and cried out again and again: "He is risen. Our Lord is risen indeed." Their brokenness was healed; their guilt was forgiven. They were like men and women released from prison; they were freed from the oppression of despair. In 1839 in Jamaica on the morning of emancipation the former slaves went up to a high hill overlooking the bay to watch the sun rise, the sun which brought them the new day and liberation. At the first rays of the sun their voices broke into a chant: "Free, free, free." The disciples knew this freedom.

Andrew went in to wake Peter and to find Thomas to tell him what had happened. Peter joined in their elation, but Thomas had disappeared. The apostles unlocked the door and went out in the streets. There was nothing to fear. They sought out the followers of Jesus who were still in the city, and they spoke out with courage. Thomas, however, was not to be found.

When they did find him, they tried to convince him of Jesus' resurrection. Thomas replied, "Unless I see the holes made in his hands by the nails and put my finger in them, and until I place my hand in his side, I will not believe." He was honest and realistic.

Thomas rejected his community. If he had remained with the others, he would have seen Jesus and been spared his terrible period of doubt and despair.

Jesus loved Thomas and would not let him go. A week later, the disciples were still meeting behind locked doors. Jesus appeared suddenly in their midst and said to Thomas, "Put your finger in the holes in my hands and your fist in the hole in my side." Jesus asked Thomas to cease his doubt and unbelief. Thomas fell to his knees and cried out, "My Lord and my God!" Jesus then replied, "You became a believer because you have seen me. Blessed are you, and blessed are those who have not seen me and have believed." This was the first time any of the disciples had realized and declared Jesus' true identity. Thomas the doubter became the first true believer.

Chapter 7

The Conversion of Thomas

The transformation of Thomas from stubborn doubt and disbelief is one of the most powerful and authentic experiences in all religious literature (Jn 20:24-29).

Thomas was one of Jesus' most courageous and faithful disciples, and Jesus addressed some of his most profound insights to Thomas. Thomas realized the danger of Jesus' going up to Jerusalem for the Passover, and he warned his beloved master. When Jesus would not listen, he said to Jesus and the other disciples, "Let us go up to the Holy City and die with him." Thomas was a realist who knew of the plots to destroy Jesus. He intended to stick by his master no matter what happened.

When Jesus was seized in the Garden of Gethsemane, it was clear that Jesus was the only one the soldiers wanted—the one who was kissed by Judas. Jesus told his disciples to put down their weapons. They obeyed him, fleeing into the night. One by one the disciples gathered in the stone hideaway which could be locked and bolted. Peter and others brought back the horrible news of Jesus' condemnation, crucifixion, and death. Thomas supported the other disciples through their agony. Their fellowship, their mutual sharing, kept them sane. They were so bound up in their own agony and fear that they did not even notice that Thomas had slipped away. The disciples fell into deep sleep just before dawn, and Thomas was gone when they awoke.

Why had Thomas slipped away? With his own strength he had supported and ministered to the others for three days. He could not see anything more that he could do. We must remember that he was strong, and he was a realist. As Thomas was sleeping, Jesus appeared to the two men traveling to Emmaus and to the disciples in their hiding place.

For those who had met the risen Jesus, everything changed. Agony gave way to ecstasy. Their hopelessness gave way to divine joy and holy awe; they could not deny what they saw and felt. They looked at one another, and they saw in each other the *same transformation that they felt in themselves*. This group experience with Jesus was more than they had dared to imagine. In his human/divine body, Jesus urged them to touch him and to feel his wounds. And then Jesus disappeared, as if the bolted door and stone wall did not exist.

From that moment, Thomas and the other disciples knew that Jesus received all who would be open to his welcoming divine arms—doubters and believers, those with great religious experiences and those who work with faith and love to spread the good news of the resurrection. Jesus can transform any of us who will steadfastly grow in fellowship. These are the real saints.

Thomas had been very close to Jesus during Jesus' ministry, and once his doubt and fear vanished he became one of the greatest Christian missionaries. Tradition tells us that he founded Christian fellowships all the way to India, where he was martyred in A.D. 54. Many writings have been attributed to him.

As I reflected on the life of Thomas, I began to see how deeply he influenced the early, growing Christian Church. Even those who have denied the reality of the resurrection can become great Christian saints, as long as they stay close to the Christian community and live with others in love and harmony.

I wondered how I could portray the magnificence of this Christian saint. A poet friend had been reflecting on the life of Thomas, and he sent me the following poem.[1] Each time I read it, I appreciate more the loving grandeur of the risen Christ and Thomas:

> I tell you straight, I am not weak in the hams
> As grown men go. I have seen strong men die,
> And the weeping and prostrate too, lambs
> Of children baffled by the pain while women
>   cry.
>
> You want a fact? Death is a fact.
> When death arrives, everything else goes,

As if an absolute and cruel king had lacked
A seat and every good man gave up his. Those

Fragrances of springtime, friendships at a feast,
One's treasure of a wife, some wealth secure,
Fresh bread, the morning birds, the psalms; all
    yeast
That leavens little pockets in the dusty world,
    as sure

And stable in the face of death as wind
Or fall's expected crops. A house of twigs. Then
    came
Our rabbi, one good man who could rescind. . .
But no, I leap ahead. With these two eyes I saw
    him heal the lame.

(By what new power?) Madmen he
    dispossessed of imps,
The blind he sighted . . . on and on. It was like joy
To be with him, to see the miseries fall flat,
    to see the crimps
He put in pain itself, just walking by,
    sweet-tempered as a boy.

Then Lazarus of Bethany fell sick and word
Was come. The Rabbi said he would not die.
Or something such. That's why we thought
    absurd
His saying two days later, staring at the sky,

"Let's to Judea." Well, you should have seen
    the bunch

Go taut. Was this another of his parables?
    Judea, mind you,
Where they think God's stones were made to
    crunch
A rabbi's bones, where most cheerfully they
    nearly slew

The only man who ever helped to set so many
    things to right.
We tried to hold him back, but nothing
    worked. He said
Some dark things touching daylight and some
    light
Ones touching sleep. Then he told us: Lazarus
    was dead.

I saw two things: that death was waiting like a
    beast
In Bethany; and death would eat our rabbi. And
    with that
The old, sad sickness of the world rose like a
    dead sun in the east
For me. I fell back on my toughness and I told
    them pat,

"Let's all go. Let's die with him." After all, if he
    dies
Life's as hopeless as it was before. You talk

about a glum
Crew: I thought (but didn't say), let's have no
    pious lies
Of Pharisees on resurrection, nor glib promises,
    but dumb

As stones themselves go all as one with him
Into the blackness. I never was more wrong. (I
    take that back.)
Still, death collapsed before his powers once
    again, and he, as trim
As a bridegroom, handed Lazarus to life. A
    godly knack,

I thought, for strewing health the way a sower
    casts
The seed. "How does he do it?" came into my
    mind
And then passed on. I've known since then that
    no idea lasts
That evidence compels. The sovereign thing to
    bind

A truth with us is some surprising way of
    putting something old,
A new fruition on the same old tree. But on.
    Time passed.
The Passover approached, the Rabbi spoke of
    death in cold
Consolement as I heard it. We shaken Twelve
    looked on aghast

To hear him say that he would die, as should
　　we all,
For some vague good I didn't catch. Now? Now
　　that death
Had cowered at his voice? And then I saw it was
　　a stall
Back there in Bethany; the monster only
　　waited, held its breath.

They took him, tried him, sold him, beat him so
Another man would plead, hung him up like
　　meat
For kites. The rest of us had gone so many turns
　　morale was low.
Our courage in exhaustion, it made a balance
　　to retreat

Or stay with him and suicide, more Roman
　　than a Jew
Would care to be. Before he left he said he went
To sweep a room for us past death. He said we
　　knew
Where he was going and would follow. I'd no
　　notion where he meant

And told him so. He said the way was he. I think
　　you know
How much that braced me up when all the
　　pebbles lay
Within the ring (as I then thought). Time
　　seemed so slow.

I'm told, the Magdalene got John and Cephas
  on the run.
They thought the body stolen. Wrong again.
  Too neat
For thieves. The men went home. The woman,
  totally undone,
Remained behind, recalling things he meant to
  her, when who should greet

Her but the gardener. To make it short, the
  gardener was not
The gardener; the Rabbi was alive, she said. I
  knew the type.
Death is such cold and slicing steel some folks
  talk rot.
To keep from going mad they dream up such
  fulfilling tripe.

As "other worlds where no one dies." That's
  what I thought
Of Mary's gardener. I wanted nothing more of
  it, or them.
The men, each time we gathered, got so
  overwrought
I had no stomach for it. I feared that if I stayed
  I'd just condemn

Them for their womanish self-accusations, so I
  stayed
Away. (My judgment never played me worse.)
  They said

He came to them past locks. Don't ask me how.
　　It's not my trade,
This thinking hard about impossibilities like
　　how the dead

Can turn around and not be dead. I laughed, of
　　course,
But they were resolute. They asked me what
　　would make
A proof to satisfy my doubts. I said, The most
　　immediate source
Of this ruinous death, his wounds. If I could
　　take

Him in my hands like any man, as well as ask
　　my eyes,
I'd say all right, have done, the world is bright
　　and sweet.
But now my curiosity was up. Next week I bore
　　their humid sighs
Behind the fastened doors. I stood staring when
　　he stepped as neat

As thinking up to me, said, "Here, in my hands,
　　the holes.
Put your fingers there in place of the nails. Here
　　in my side,
Make your hand the spear. Believe!" I looked
　　at Cephas and our roles
Look switched to me. Time was I could hardly
　　abide

His fawning, calling him Messiah, Lord.
Now I was there. If Cephas was a fool, the same
    fool I.
I saw it now: the monster sprang and ate; its
    victim's sword
Cut deep and wide within so that, through
    dying, death should die.

It was too good to be. And yet it was. This was
    the man
Who died, and here he was alive, and teaching
    me good sense.
I thought back on the healings and my short
    attention span,
The way the signs became more obvious for
 those more dense

Like me and, as He waited for my reply, my legs
Gave way, my eyes dissolved, I lost track of my
    hands,
My breathing came in gusts, and I admitted, as
    a blind man begs,
That He was God, asked His forgiveness, while
    the lands

Convulsed in evil's long, reptilian and dying
    throes.
And now, remembering it all, I lust to live again
Those subtler signs: Lazarus, the blind man, the
    touching of His clothes.

Or better yet, to not have eyed Him, just be
told through other men.

Chapter 8

Jesus Meets with his Disciples

So often we forget that the risen Jesus remained in human bodily form for over thirty days. He went where the need was greatest. We do not have an extended account of which disciples he was with, but in John's Gospel we do have one account of a significant meeting with a group of disciples who had not yet understood the meaning of their mission. We get an idea of how Jesus must have reached out to his other followers by the way he met and guided the disciples who were fishing in the Sea of Galilee several days after the resurrection. He entered into their lives and met their needs. First of all he showed them where the fish were, just as he had done early in his ministry. Then he fed the hungry fishermen, who had toiled all night long. And then he made clear to them how they should treat one another.

For several weeks Jesus had made appearances—to his mother; to James, a member of his family; to each of the disciples; and then to five hundred of the brothers and sisters at one time. We have only Paul's record of these meetings, and we cannot describe these encounters in detail (1 Cor 5:3-11). Shortly before he left his disciples, though, he came to seven of them again at the Sea of Galilee, and John's Gospel describes this event quite thoroughly. For me, John's account presents the very essence of what the disciples experienced as they met the resurrected Jesus of Nazareth.[1]

Several disciples gathered at the Sea of Tiberias, the Roman name for the Sea of Galilee. The Gospel of John is very specific (as the beloved disciple often is) about those present: Simon Peter was there, and with him was Thomas the Twin, whose story we have just heard. Nathanael from Cana-in-Galilee, the two sons of Zebedee (James and John), and two other unnamed disciples rounded out the group.

They were no longer grieving. Life had come together for them, but they had not yet realized the full significance of what they had experienced. The world-shattering meaning of Jesus' rising from the dead had not occurred to them. They were alive and whole, but they didn't see how much the whole world needed to hear and experience the hope they had received and the transformation they had undergone. They had not yet grasped the necessity of sharing what they had experienced; they did not realize that this event was the hope of the whole world.

A fishing expedition can be very healing, but it is not exactly the activity to be expected of people who had been rescued from utter despair by the most important

event in history. Late in the afternoon Peter an-
nounced to the group that he was going fishing; the
others, most of them probably Galilean fisherfolk, replied that they would go with him. They wasted no
time getting their nets ready and launching the boat.
Throughout the night they cast out their nets, but they
caught nothing, nothing. I have always marveled at the
persistence and dedication of fisherfolk. They get up in
the middle of the night to fish at the best time; they
travel hundreds of miles and never seem to get discouraged. I have often thought how alive and vital Christianity would be if the ordinary Christian had the
self-sacrificing devotion of run-of-the-mill fisherfolk.

Dawn was already breaking, and the first rays of the
sun were beginning to reveal the superb beauty of the
Sea of Galilee and the timbered hills around it. Jesus
stood alone on the empty beach. The fishermen were
heading back toward the shore. They saw a man standing there, but they did not recognize that it was Jesus.
He called out to them: "Hey there, you lads, have you
caught anything?" It is important for us to hear the
natural, common, ordinary way with which the risen
Jesus spoke to his friends. His manner had nothing
stilted about it. We also need to remember that these
were young men; the Greek can mean nothing else. Jesus was in his very early thirties, according to incarnational time, and most of his companions were about his
age. None were older than their late thirties and one
perhaps was in his early twenties. Speaking as one in
my eighties, I know that I have learned much in the last
twenty-five years, but I have also realized that there is a

dedication, energy, and power in young men and women touched by the risen Jesus that older people often do not have. Would Christianity have spread like a mountain fire over the ancient world had most of Jesus' disciples been in their sixties?

As a group the young men called back: "No." To their straightforward and discouraged reply, Jesus shouted back: "Shoot the net to the starboard, and you will make a catch." Jesus knew fishing and fishermen. There was no particular reason not to make one more try after fishing all night, so out went the net. The men began to haul it in, and they were struck with terror. They could not even haul in all the fish the net enclosed.

John was the first to make the connection. He remembered the catch of fish when they first met Jesus, the haul which touched Peter so deeply. John spoke softly to Peter: "It is the Lord." This statement was all that Simon Peter needed to come to his senses. Impulsive, action-oriented Peter tucked some clothes into his belt and threw himself into the water and swam to shore. The other disciples brought the boat to land, towing the net full of fish behind them. They were only about a hundred yards from shore.

The Fourth Gospel seldom refers to John by name, but rather calls him the beloved disciple or the disciple whom Jesus loved. I am much touched by this practice. Each of us is indeed the beloved disciple. The more we need Jesus, the more he loves us and the more beloved we are. He longs to deliver us from evil and darkness, to heal us and bring us to eternal life.

When the fishermen had beached the boat, they climbed out onto the shore. A charcoal fire was burning, with some fish and bread roasting on it. More was needed if they were all to eat, and so Jesus told them, "Bring some of the fish that you have caught just now." Peter, still dripping wet, jumped onto the boat and dragged ashore the net bulging with large fish, 153 of them. And the net was not even torn.

This narrative sets my mind and imagination on fire. Just as Jesus had broken through the dullness of his disciples' minds with the miraculous catch at the beginning of his ministry, so now he uses his godly power, his heightened human capacity, to bring the disciples to themselves. There is nothing wrong with this kind of human capacity as long as it is used for the right purpose, in the service of resurrected love. When the disciples had marveled at the first great catch of fish, Jesus had told them they would become fishers of human beings. This later resurrection narrative marks the fully implemented call of these men to become evangelists, followers of Christ, men and women who were to bring the good news of God's present kingdom to hungry and thirsty people all over the world.

The precise number of the fish is a delightful fisherman's touch. We would be hard pressed to find an angler ignorant of the number of a catch or of their weight and length. It was indeed a truly remarkable catch! Much time and energy has been spent looking for allegorical and hidden meanings to this number, but I am simply impressed with the characteristic fisherfolk touch.

Jesus reveals his practical and down-to-earth response to his friends' actual situation. They were hungry and tired. They had toiled all night. First of all, he took care of their creaturely needs. He was interested in their immediate, physical human needs; he was concerned not just for human souls but for hungering human beings. It is impossible to bring the full message of Jesus Christ, risen, to people who are in poverty and oppression by inner or outer powers until we show an interest in their human needs.

The men counted the fish, and cleaned some of them and placed them on the grill. Everyone was silent. They knew that this mysterious man was Jesus, their friend, master and Lord, but there was something uncanny about him, something numinous. Not one of them dared to ask who he was. They knew, but they could think of no way of opening a conversation. After a few moments Jesus broke their awed silence with homey familiarity: "Come and have your breakfast." Then Jesus came over, took the bread, and gave it to them. He did the same with the fish. A wineskin was brought out and this was passed around. A fishing trip without a wineskin was unthinkable. The ice was broken, and they began to talk with one another and with Jesus. The longer they talked the more comfortable they became.

A Eucharist by the Sea

I can imagine being there with the disciples and Jesus. No one doubted that this was the same person with whom they had trudged up and down Palestine, the same person who drove the moneychangers out of the temple, the same physical being who had been flogged and hung on the cross. The wounds could still be seen in his hands and feet. Still there was something more here; the disciples all experienced what three of them had encountered at the transfiguration. They just didn't know how to respond. There was both community and transformation. True holiness is awesome, and people with sense don't treat it casually.

They would never forget that meal together, with the rising sun warming their bodies, and the bread, fish, and wine filling their stomachs and their souls. They remembered only too clearly their last meal together before this one: This meal by the Sea of Galilee redeemed the unfulfilled promises of stout loyalty made at the Passover meal. On that sad night, Jesus had told them to continue having communal meals together, and he had made vague, veiled allusions to the bread and wine being his body and blood.

Now they understood. How could they ever again bless bread and wine and take them without thinking of these two quite different meals together? They discovered as the years rolled on that Jesus was still present with them when they broke the bread and shared the cup with one another. The Jesus who came to the disciples with the rising sun at the shore of the Sea of Tiberias was indeed the dayspring from on high. He continued to come to the disciples and to other men and women who had been gripped by Jesus' resurrection victory over crucifixion and death. Christians throughout the ages have experienced the presence of the risen Christ in their eucharistic celebrations and as they have turned inward in need and affection and opened the door to the one knocking there.

A Lesson in Caring

When they had finished their breakfast, Jesus went up to Peter and suggested that they walk alone by the shore of the lake. Peter was both anxious and glad to have this time alone with his master. He felt forgiven, but had he forgiven himself entirely? As they walked along, Jesus spoke directly to Peter: "Simon, son of John, do you love me as much as you professed the night I was betrayed? Do you really love me more than these others as you then said?" Peter was embarrassed and simply replied, "Yes, Lord, you know that I love you." And then Jesus told him: "Feed my lambs." To Peter these words were filled with meaning. As he ministered with forgiveness to those as weak and poor in spirit as he was, Peter would be feeding the lambs. He would feed them with the good news of resurrection, love, and forgiveness. And as he did this, his guilt would be washed away.

They walked on a little further, and Jesus repeated his question a second time: "Simon, son of John, do you love me?" Peter again replied: "Yes, Lord, you know that I love you." Jesus replied again: "Then take care of my sheep." And Peter understood what Jesus was saying. He had been a leader of their small band, been called the Rock (Peter), and now he was told to take care of the growing fellowship. The Greek word used here means far more than *feeding;* it means the general care of the sheep—seeking out the lost, arranging for their safety and well-being, caring for their total welfare.

And then Jesus spoke a third time: "Simon, son of John, do you love me?" Peter was deeply touched and hurt by the doubt that Jesus' third question implied. Peter remembered all too clearly how he had denied his master three times and had given Jesus just cause for doubting Peter. Peter's face told as much as the words he spoke. His eyes watered with tears as he thought back on the bitter weeping of that night of denial: "Lord, you know everything, the depth of my human heart and all of me; you know very well that I love you." Jesus answered much as he had before: "Then feed my little sheep." Jesus did not need to question Peter further. The three denials were undone. Instead, he went on to predict Simon's utter faithfulness, even to death; Peter would give up his own self-centered way and allow love and the Spirit to lead him. Jesus brought this dramatic encounter and commissioning to a close with two final words: "Follow me."

A Humbling Personal Lesson in Loving

Our second son John had not yet learned to read during fifth grade. After considering all the possibilities, we finally settled on a remedial school. Our son had asked to go to a private school, but he disliked the one we chose for him. It was an excellent school, and the first thing they did was to administer a battery of tests.

Then I found myself in the unusual position of being on the other side of the table, with the counselor asking me, "Do you have any idea what this child's problem is?" I replied that I didn't know of any reason other than stubbornness and obstinacy for John's problem. And then he dropped the bombshell: "The problem with this child is that he doesn't think that you really care for him or love him."

I protested vigorously that whenever I tried to show him love, warmth, and affection, he pushed me away. The counselor continued, "Has it ever occurred to you why he pushes you away? He is testing you to see how much you really do love him."

"At eleven years of age?" I asked.

"Even at eleven."

I decided on the spot that I was going to love that child if it killed me. And it did kill part of me. We went horseback riding together. Even though I have the manual dexterity of a palsied hippopotamus, I tried to do woodworking with him and other hands-on activities which he enjoyed. The real turnaround, however, came one day in a motel on the oceanfront at Laguna Beach. I came into his room one morning and asked, "Johnnie, wouldn't you like to go swimming with me?" Then, as only an eleven-year-old can say it, he replied, "Nah, I'd rather watch television."

In the past when I got this kind of response I would leave feeling rejected to spend my time doing something I would have preferred doing anyway. But after the counselor's revelation, I thought to myself, "Perhaps he is only testing me; I'll keep my sense of humor and pursue him." In a very playful manner (and this attitude was most important) I capered over to the TV set and turned it off. We tussled around the room, out the door, down the stairs, around the corner, out on the walkway, and down into the ocean.

Do you know what that child said as we emerged from the first wave? He blew the water from his nose and exclaimed, "Father, I wondered how long it would take you to do this."

The old pattern was broken, and we began to relate. His Iowa tests went up three years in six months' time. He began to learn to read, but don't think that this was the end of the struggle. One day as we were sitting beside a pool in Arizona where he was living (he was nineteen at the time), he spoke to me calmly and deliberately: "Father, you know, I have never liked you very well." This was not what my bruised ego needed at that moment, but I remembered I was going to try to show love. I remembered what the headmaster of a school told parents to do when their children said that they did not like them. I replied, "John, I don't blame you; there are many times when I don't like me either."

From that moment, things between us mutated to a new level. A year or so later, John was with me at a conference I was giving. I decided to tell the story I have just related; I wanted to hear his response. On the way to the place where we were staying that night, John spoke up: "Father, did I actually say that?" I nodded my assent.

The next morning as we were breakfasting, John initiated the conversation with, "I remember when I made

up my mind that I would never ask you for anything
again in my life." I asked him to tell me about it.

"I was seven years old. You had been reading A.
Conan Doyle's *Tale of Sherlock Holmes* to my brother
and me." He could even remember the author and the
book. "My brother was away for several days, but I
wanted you to read aloud to me anyway; and so I
brought you the book and asked you to read. You said
that you were too busy. I brought the book the next
night, and you again said you were too busy. The same
thing happened on the third night, and quite con-
sciously I made up my mind that I would never ask *you*
for anything else again in my life."

I had not realized how sensitive and needy of my love
and attention this son of mine was. My refusal to read
had struck at him as effectively as if I had wielded a
club. I, of course, did not even remember the incident.
However, patient love can even restore the years which
the locusts have eaten; and a deep and real relationship
finally developed between us.

In 1981 my wife Barbara was badly injured on the
docks of Yokohama. When her condition was stabi-
lized, she was flown home to Los Angeles. Thus John
and I lived together for the two months that she was in
the hospital. During that time, we came to know each
other in a closer and more creative way than we ever
had before. I kept house for him while sharing his
apartment.

When Barbara was finally released from the hospital
and she and I went to stay with close friends, I found a
card from him addressed to me. On the front was a pic-

ture of an iguana. Inside was this message: "I guana miss you." We had come a long way, John and I, and we were truly bonded.

A few years later, John and I took a trip together. He had an appointment with a friend who was helping sort out his childhood. He stopped to call this friend so they could talk. He came back in tears; his friend had told him that I could take any of the pain of his childhood, and that pain burst forth. I had to drive. John was purified in a way, and he was as frank as he had ever been. He could tell me anything and know that I would accept him.

Later on John became seriously ill. He called for us to come to be with him in Hawaii. When I asked, "When?" he replied "Tomorrow." We dropped everything. We were thus able to have five months of ministering to each other through his fatal illness. This shared time made us both realize how deeply we are bound to one another. John died after this very special time together. As his body left for his final home, these words sprang to mind: "Now cracks a noble heart. Good night, sweet prince and flights of angels sing thee to thy rest."

John and I had developed the closest kind of fellowship. He had no fear; he KNEW that he was about to set out upon a new religious journey. His faith supported mine. This is another example of the power of shared fellowship and love.

It is love and the fellowship of family and community which brings people to wholeness. Jesus gives us the signs which lead us on that pathway.

Telling the Story Another Way

Trying to reach people in our Western world with the good news of the crucified and risen Jesus of Nazareth can be very discouraging. So many of us have been inoculated with a debased, moralistic version of Christianity that we have become immune to the real thing. We are part of a civilization—although traditionally Christian—that has little understanding of the mercy, power and love of God. Secular people turn away with scorn from a Christianity they do not understand, without investigating it. Liberal Christians have often deleted the mystery and power of the gospel and reduced it to an impossible moral imperative or to self-propelled social action. Some conservative Christians are so frightened that they cling to the letter of the text and forget that the risen Jesus is still very much with us in the power and love of the Holy Spirit. They can become dominating and authoritarian rather than loving and nurturing.

How can we get by these barriers and tend and feed both the lambs and sheep? By telling the story in another way. Few people have done it better than C. S. Lewis in his children's tale, *The Lion, the Witch and the Wardrobe*. When we get people truly to hear the Christian story, it still has incredible power. When it touches us and transforms us, we know its truth.

One very sophisticated and agnostic graduate student in counseling psychology at Notre Dame read *The Lion, the Witch and the Wardrobe* in my class on death, dying, and suffering. It seeped past her rejection of

Christianity and let her deal with the reality of Jesus' resurrection. This lightened the darkness and tragedy of human suffering and death and opened the possibility of belief for her. Many years ago I had a similar experience reading this book to my twelve-year-old daughter. When I finished she said, "Why, Father, that is the story of Jesus and Easter, isn't it?" No version of the gospel story I know would have touched off that kind of interest and response, and it has stayed with her even as she is now a grandmother. I have told the story before, but a good story always bears retelling.

Four children in wartime Britain are boarded in the country in an old and rambling house. They discover a wardrobe in one of the rooms through which they can pass into another dimension of time and space—into Narnia, which is ruled by the White Witch. She is the epitome of evil, and under her rule it is always December and never Christmas. One of the children, Edmund, turns traitor over some candy and betrays the others to the White Witch.

All is lost until Aslan, a numinous lion, appears and rescues the country by his power. However, he can save the traitor Edmund only by offering himself as a ransom for him. And so Aslan dies and Edmund is set free. It seems as though the end to all hope has come when Aslan is destroyed; there is, however, a deeper magic from beyond the dawn of time which states that those who give their lives for others, expecting nothing in return, cannot really die. The lion Aslan rises from the dead.

There, shining in the sunrise, larger than they had seen him before, shaking his mane . . . stood Aslan himself.

"Aren't you dead, then, dear Aslan?" said Lucy. . . .

"Do I look it?"

"But what does it all mean?" asked Susan when they were somewhat calmer.

"It means," said Aslan, "that though the witch knew the Deep Magic, there is a magic deeper still which she did not know. Her knowledge goes back only to the dawn of Time. But if she could have looked a little further back, into the stillness and the darkness before Time dawned, she would have read there a different incantation. She would have known that when a willing victim who had committed no treachery was killed in a traitor's stead the Table would crack and Death itself would start working backwards."[2]

What Does All This Mean?

If Jesus truly lived, died and rose again, if the resurrection is historical reality, what difference does it make? All the difference in the world. Indeed, if the resurrection of Jesus is true, we are confronted head-on with the fact of a caring spiritual reality; we are face to face with so much of importance that it is truly difficult to believe all that this event means. The implications of Jesus' resurrection are almost too good to be true.

First of all, the risen Jesus' meeting with his friends tells us in the most striking way possible that there is more to reality than just energy and mass. Spirit is real as well and has ultimate significance. We human beings share in the reality of spirit as well as of matter, just as Jesus did. We are both body and spirit, matter and soul; both were created by God and both are good. We need both in order to come to our fulfillment as amphibious human beings. The resurrection speaks to the essential unity of the physical and spiritual in our universe.

This physical body of ours can die and disintegrate, and yet a part of us continues on and can rise in a new form. We have the potential of continued life, just as a tiny, dying redwood seed can give birth to a gigantic tree. Human beings had dreamed of this possibility, had hoped for it, but in the resurrection humanity's imperishability and potential for transformation were revealed before many witnesses. Those who killed Jesus did not destroy him. There was something more to him than just a body, and there is something more to us than our physicality. How differently we look at life when the resurrection of Jesus raises and expands our horizons and our consciousness. We have an eternal destiny, whether we like it or not. This can be either good news or bad news.

What good would eternal life be, life that continues forever beyond the grave, if the world on the other side is simply a continuation of this one? We would then be immersed forever in a realm of existence in which evil

and ugliness, power and selfishness, hostility and destructiveness were ultimate factors. If eternal life were
to be a continuation of the suffering and tragedy, the
cruelty and sorrow, the futility and bitterness that so
many in our world know, then it would be far better
just to cease to exist. Under those circumstances, death
and extinction would be a blessed relief.

But the resurrection of Jesus tells us that evil has
been conquered, that it is not part of the ultimate nature of things, that it is derivative and not on an equal
footing with the loving God. The resurrection is the
showing forth in the arena of this physical world that
God wins, goodness wins, love conquers. The best human being was confronted by the hatred, greed, and
bigotry of the world. The forces of self-centeredness
and evil condemned Jesus of Nazareth, judged him,
crucified him; they watched and mocked him as he
died. They appeared to be victorious, but God raised
Jesus from the dead. The risen Jesus demonstrated the
victory of what he embodied—love, meaning, hope,
joy, peace, transformation, never-ending growth.

As I have already pointed out, it is impossible for us
to understand why evil exists and has such power. But
the resurrection declares that evil will not always tri-
umph, as it does so often now. In the end we can enter
God's kingdom and find continuing new life; this kingdom will eventually come upon our earth as in heaven,
but we do not need to wait for this. We can start now
on the path toward new and fuller life, which is manifested in the risen Jesus. In the following chapter I will
give several different ways by which we can enter now

upon this new life. We need not be under the domina-
tion of evil; we can be free of its befouling control. The
risen Christ is available *now* and can free us from that
which seeks to destroy us.

The most difficult part of the resurrection message
for me to believe is that God in Christ did all this for us
long before we did anything worthy of this kind of love.
Christ died, rose again, and comes to us now not because we are worthy of God, but *simply because God loves
us as we are.* God is seeking us out just as Jesus picked
out his disciples and friends and then sought them out
after his resurrection to bring them back to life. The
greater our needs, the greater God's effort to find us,
who are like the prodigal, the elder brother, and the
straying sheep. The resurrection reveals the loving and
seeking God, who would find us and transform us so we
may achieve our divine potential. What greater gift can
we receive? We need simply to cease running away and
to receive the grace upon grace that the Risen Lord
holds in his hands for us.

There are three more acts in our drama, and now we
turn to these. Through them the resurrection is univer-
salized and made available to all.

Chapter 9

Ascension

In the weeks after Passover Sunday, there was a great change in the way Jesus appeared to his friends and followers, most clearly recorded in the Gospel of Luke. Mark does not speak of this change at all, and in John's first account of the resurrection Jesus speaks to Mary Magdalene in the garden and refers in the present tense to his ascending to the Father. (There is no other specific reference to ascension in John's Gospel.) The final words of Matthew's Gospel speak of Jesus gathering his disciples together on a mountain in Galilee, giving them a commission to preach the gospel all over the world, and giving them authority on earth and in heaven. In this account Jesus' physical departure is only implied. Luke, however, clearly differentiates the resurrection, the physical departure of Jesus from his disciples and this ordinary world, and his giving them the Holy Spirit to empower them. When Jesus ascends to the Father, he will send the Comforter to guide and stand by them. The Comforter (paraclete) cannot fully come until Jesus ascends to the Father.

Undoubtedly these events were closely related. We are dealing with the holy in its most numinous form, and it is difficult to clearly differentiate the various aspects of Jesus' victory over death and evil. John tells of Jesus' coming to his disciples, breathing on them, and giving them the Holy Spirit; the same gift is implied again in the final passage of Matthew. Jesus also speaks of giving them the Comforter when he is no longer with them physically. For some of those who had experienced a meeting with the risen Jesus, the experience gave them hope in and conviction about Jesus' victory. For others the meeting contained a quality of finality and farewell. For still others the experience was one of receiving a new spiritual energy. For some all three meanings were united in one overwhelming experience, while others experienced these three meanings as separate consecutive experiences. The Church has espoused the separation of these three experiences as recorded in Luke, and from this account religious practice and theology have developed.

The Church separated the final encounters with Jesus into three different kinds of events: Jesus' rising from death illustrates his victory over death and reveals the divine meaning of his life; the ascension of Jesus refers to Jesus' return to the Father so his presence would be available to all human beings everywhere; the gift of the Holy Spirit at Pentecost tells of a new kind of presence of Jesus and God within his followers which empowers them to live out their destiny in a hostile world.

There was a period in my religious life when I was embarrassed by the feast of the Ascension. The Church treated it as one of the great days of the Christian year, and yet Luke pictured the event in a way that made very little sense to me. The same picture is portrayed in much religious art: Jesus stepped onto a cloud and was whisked away up there into the sky, into heaven. The picture seemed ridiculous, like the ending of a naïve, old-fashioned, sentimental novel. After all, from a round earth, which way is up? Evidently the Russian cosmonauts shared the view that heaven was supposed to be "up there"; they reassured their Marxist government that they did not find God or heaven on their journey into space. Nonetheless, Ascension Day is ranked along with Christmas, Pentecost, Easter and All Saints Day as one of the great days of the Church year.

One value of the liturgical year is that when we follow that year it forces us to deal with the great mysteries of the Christian faith. I began to ponder the account given in Luke and to meditate over it. Out of the depth of this reflection I realized that there is deep religious significance to the experience Luke describes. We do not have to link ourselves with biblical literalists who expect Jesus to return momentarily on the same kind of cloud on which he supposedly departed. We don't have to go off on a mountain to stand gazing into the heavens awaiting his return.

What actually happened to the disciples? And why is that great experience described as the ascension still of abiding and crucial importance to us today? So often our language is inadequate when we try to tell people what has happened to us in our most indescribable religious experiences. Small-particle physicists cannot describe what they experience in the heart of the atom. Great art is required to give a hint of a glorious sunset over the cliff at the seashore, and only great poetry can express the full depth of human love. Our difficulties in communication are particularly marked when we try to tell others of transforming religious experiences. In *The Doors of Perception*, Aldous Huxley has pointed out that most European languages are very poor in words expressing spiritual experience. We can begin to communicate our experience of the numinous to another who has had a similar experience, but if our experience is unknown to the other then sharing becomes extremely difficult, if not impossible. If the ascension was a unique, experiential religious *fact*, then it is dreadfully difficult to communicate.

In addition to these difficulties, we have to describe our experiences in terms of the frame of reference or the worldview of which we are a part. Many different worldviews have existed through the ages and even today. In the time of Jesus of Nazareth, when people were observed to be acting in a completely irrational or uncharacteristic way, they were described as "demon possessed": One or more demons were said to have possessed their inner being. Now we describe these weird behaviors as insanity or mental derangement, or possession by autonomous psychological trauma, *or* by a psychic or spiritual reality taking over the conscious personality. But whether we call that reality a demon or an autonomous complex makes little difference if we understand that both terms refer to the same reality. A negative spiritual reality is most certainly involved in most cases of depression, anxiety, and other psychological disturbances.

Most Biblical writers saw the sun and the stars go around the earth and believed that the earth was the center of the universe; everything went around it. We now realize that lots of things are going around, including the earth. We describe the same experience, but we use different language. Similarly, if we return home to be confronted with a house in chaos, the drawers pulled out and the contents strewn about the floor, we could infer that a thief has been there; however, if there was a two-year-old left free in the house we would be more likely to attribute the disorder to the child. Our interpretive viewpoint, in other words, shapes our way of describing the phenomena we encounter.

The disciples expressed the overwhelming numinous experience of being with the physical, risen Jesus for the last time in the only way available to them. The experience overwhelmed them. The King of Kings was going home to his own kingdom. After a blaze of ineffable glory, he was in a bodily form with them no more.

Let us put ourselves back into the world and experience of Jesus' time. These people lived in a relatively simple universe. At the center was the earth, saucerlike; inverted over it was the sky, like a huge bowl. On top of the bowl was heaven. They also believed that souls were a kind of substance like an invisible gas, which departed from the body at death. The purer souls, like a rarer gas, went up quickly through the skies to heaven. Impurer and blemished souls rose only a little way to one of the lesser heavens and remained flitting about the earth annoying people or (misfortune of misfortunes) sank through the earth into hell itself.

Many of the ancients believed that there were many degrees of heaven and that people received their just deserts by going to the first, seventh, or tenth heaven depending on the purity of their souls. When the disciples were separated *physically* from their Risen Lord, who existed in incandescent magnificence, how could they have explained it other than that Jesus had ascended into heaven?

We in our quite different time might have described the same experience as his breaking through into another dimension of reality, or as the door between the worlds being flung open, bathing us with heaven's brilliance. We would be expressing the same experience but using different descriptions due to our different worldview. Sadly, those who don't believe in anything but the physical simply dismiss the resurrection and the ascension of Jesus as nonsense because they have no place for the experience. Someone close to me once said: "Morton, if I had a worldview which allowed it, I would be very religious, because I have tremendous religious experiences. But since there is no place in my universe for them, I pay no attention to them."

Luke gave us two descriptions of what happened to the disciples in this critical experience of joyous separation: one at the end of his gospel, the other at the beginning of the second and continuing volume about Jesus and Christianity, the Acts of the Apostles. Luke's Gospel concludes with these words: "Jesus led them out to a spot near Bethany and blessed them with uplifted hands; in the act of blessing he was separated from them and they returned to Jerusalem with great joy, and spent all their time in the temple glorifying God" (Lk 24:50-52). It is notable that in this account there is no mention of clouds or ascending. We find these details in Luke's other version. In Acts, Luke wrote that Jesus appeared for forty days after his resurrection, confirming his followers' experience of his resurrection and teaching them about the kingdom of God. Then Jesus met them one final time and spoke of the gift of the Holy Spirit soon to be poured out upon them. They still did not understand the full significance of his preaching and asked when Israel would come into its own sovereignty. Jesus told them directly not to worry about dates and times.

"When he had said this, as they watched, he was lifted up, and a cloud took him out of their sight. While they were gazing intently into heaven while he was leaving, there suddenly stood beside them two men in white who said: 'Men of Galilee, why are you standing there gazing into heaven? This Jesus, who has been taken up from you into heaven, will come in the same way as you saw him go into heaven.' Then they returned from the mount of Olivet, which is only a Sabbath day's journey from Jerusalem. . . . Entering the city they went to an upstairs room where they were staying. . . . All of these were constantly at prayer together and with them were a group of women, including Mary, the Mother of Jesus, and others of his family" (Acts 1:6-14).

The "rising up" of Jesus is secondary to a magnificent parting. Jesus was also hidden by a cloud on the mount of transfiguration, where in the presence of God Jesus was transformed. The pillar of cloud was one manifestation of God in the Old Testament. James Kirsch has written in depth about the significance of the cloud as divine manifestation in his book, *The Reluctant Prophet*.[1] So the use of cloud imagery is simply Luke's way of expressing that the disciples had experienced the reality of the divine in a remarkable way.

Parting without Sorrow

The strangest part of Luke's account of this parting is his description not of the beholders' experience but rather of their reaction to it. We have heard this story so many times that we fail to realize its unusualness. Would we expect his disciples to part from their Lord with great joy? Would we have expected them to take leave of the one they had loved more than life itself and proceed to Jerusalem with *great joy* and to remain in joyous prayer and praise after that? Had I been making up this story I would probably have written: "And leaving the mount of Olivet with their eyes running with tears, they said to one another, 'It was a wonderful experience while it lasted. It will be lonely as we await his return. So sad, so strange the days that are no more.' Then they went back with heavy hearts and grim determination to the tasks Jesus had appointed them to do."

In the story of the translation or ascension of Elijah, we find the natural human reaction to such a separation under quite similar circumstances. As Elijah was carried away into heaven in the chariot of fire, Elisha, who was his disciple, companion, and friend, cried out, "My father, my father, the chariots of Israel and the horsemen thereof." Then, in a typical Hebrew expression of profound grief, he ripped apart his clothes.

Jesus of Nazareth is the only great religious hero in history for whom no elegy has ever been written and no dirge ever sung. Indeed, this lack of sadness is the key to understanding the significance of the parting of the Lord from his disciples. The disciples had lost nothing. Similarly, the early Christians never spoke of *remembering* Jesus. He was for them a present reality; he was continually with them.

The continuing resurrection experiences had as one of their purposes the preparing of the disciples for separation from the physical Jesus. In many of Jesus' appearances, he was known as much by spiritual intuition as by ordinary sensory experience. In the garden, Mary recognized Jesus not by sight at first, but by the inflection of his voice. On the road to Emmaus the disciples reported that their hearts had burned within them, but they did not recognize Jesus until he broke bread before them. Experiences like these trained the followers of Jesus to know him by spiritual perception.

The resurrected Jesus appeared suddenly and then disappeared in the same way. Perhaps their Risen Lord was trying to train them to be constantly aware of his presence, to be spiritually on tiptoe. Jesus' strange comings and goings fostered this kind of awareness. Since the disciples never knew when he would be present with them or in their midst, they came to think of his presence in every conversation, at every meeting with a friend, accompanying every thought. They became constantly open to his presence. They came to rely on their spiritual apprehension of him as well as on their physical perception. These meetings lasted only until his followers were convinced of his resurrection and of his never-failing presence. Finally he parted from them with a promise that something more was to be given them.

The early Christians looked upon the parting not as a loss, but as the final confirmation of Jesus' victory, the affirmation of the incarnation and resurrection. That which had come physically into the world now departed, taking humanness into heaven and making it divine. The incarnate Son of God was returning to the Godhead, from which he came. This was the final and complete vindication of everything that he had lived, taught, and died for. From now on his presence would not be localized in one spot or time; his life assumed a cosmic nature. He became infinitely available, just like God. The disciples' numinous parting from Jesus did not mean that their friend and master was gone, but that he would now be with them even when they were scattered over the face of the earth; he was now always with them. Paul wrote: "What can separate us from the love of Christ? . . . For I am convinced that nothing in death or life, in the cosmic realm of spirits, or spiritual powers both good and evil, or in the natural human world as it is or as it shall become, in the rising and setting of the stars, or in anything else in all creation, can separate us from the love of God in Christ Jesus our Lord"(Rom 8:35-39).

Had some modern person stood with the disciples at the joyful parting with the risen Jesus, the experience would probably have been expressed in words like those of Howard Chandler Robbins:

> And have the bright immensities
>   Received our risen Lord,
> Where light-years frame the Pleiades
>   And point Orion's sword?
> Do flaming suns his footsteps trace
>   Through corridors sublime,
> The Lord of interstellar space
>   And conqueror of time?
>
> The heaven that hides him from our sight
>   Knows neither near nor far:
> An altar candle sheds its light
>   As surely as a star;
> And where his loving people meet
>   To share the gift divine,
> There stands he with unhurrying feet;
>   There heavenly splendors shine.[2]

An Essential Part of the Drama

Sometimes the action of a drama may seem irrele-
vant until we come to the end of the play. When the
glorious parting of the risen Jesus is separated entirely
from the rest of the divine drama, it makes little sense.
But when this act of the play is understood in the pro-
gression of incarnation, death, resurrection, and the
pouring forth of divine gifts at Pentecost, the feast day
which is inadequately described as the Ascension is essential to the action.

First of all, as the early Christians went out to preach
the gospel, they preached the good news of the resurrection of Jesus. The question would have inevitably
risen from those who listened to them: And where is Jesus now if he has risen from the dead? There are times
when I wish that he were around physically so I could
make a trip and consult him, but God was far wiser; we
need to learn to depend not only on our physical senses
but on the other sense of our souls, which are not
bound to the earth. Without the divine parting, the
cosmic return, Christ could have been a world power
and Christianity could have been a power game; our
freedom would have been taken from us. God loves us
too much to take our freedom from us.

This final magnificent experience of the physically
risen Jesus also taught his followers to develop their
spiritual lives. The risen Jesus had now assumed a cosmic stature and was available as people came to eucharist, turned in quiet to commune with him on the other
side of silence, or called out in sickness, need, or perse-

cution to the One who saves. They were then open to the spontaneous divine manifestations that God continually gives us in the Pentecostal experience, in dreams, in revelations, visions, and healings. This experience prepared them for his continual presence with them.

Indeed, the ascension of Jesus, the overwhelming experience of the divine return, is the inevitable result of the incarnation and the necessary preparation for the outpouring of the divine gifts at Pentecost. This final experience of the risen Jesus was for the disciples a door between the worlds, and it reaffirmed their belief that Jesus was God in the flesh. It also prepared them for another ineffable experience, which they described as the coming of the Holy Spirit.

Jesus did not just disappear. He called his family, disciples, and friends together to let them know his love for them. Christianity is not a solitary religion but a social one. No lover would disappear without saying "Goodbye" and letting them know that his love for them is endless. And because of this endless outpouring of love, Jesus' followers were called to share the love with each other. Jesus, being human as well as divine, also wanted to be with his family and friends before he left.

Chapter 10

A New Incarnation—The Coming of the Holy Spirit

In the past eighty years the importance of Pentecost and the outpouring of the Holy Spirit has been much more appreciated in Western Christendom than it formerly had been. For many years Western Christianity had been almost binatarian in practice; in actual devotional life God the Creator and Jesus the Redeemer were frequently invoked, but little attention was paid to the third person of the Trinity, the Holy Spirit. Although the Greek Orthodox Church maintained emphasis on the Paraclete (John's name for the Holy Spirit), Western churches did not. At the turn of the twentieth century, however, Pentecostal churches were founded, and they grew rapidly, because many people discovered that there was a life and power available to

Christians that many of the mainline Western Christian churches had forgotten.

In the past thirty years, this understanding spread to many Protestant denominations. And early in his papacy, in *Humanae Salutis*, Pope John XXIII called for people to pray that the Holy Spirit might renew the Roman Catholic Church and so prepare for the Second Vatican Council. The charismatic movement emphasizing the reality and empowerment of the Holy Spirit then began to spread like wildfire in a renewed Catholic Church.[1]

So much has been written in recent times about the Holy Spirit that it may seem presumptuous to devote one short chapter to the subject. A large portion of my writing has been devoted to studying the effects of the Holy Spirit as it touches and transforms the lives of human beings throughout the ages right up to the present time.[2] The basic idea of this renewal movement is that God still acts in the lives of Christians today, as the Holy Spirit did among the Christians described in the Acts of the Apostles and the letters of Paul. From the point of view of the first Christians, the action of God in our world did not cease with the ascension of Jesus. After this event the disciples and apostles were given a new spiritual life and energy, a new spiritual companion who operated within and through them and made different people of them.

Something of a momentous nature happened to the followers of Jesus at Pentecost. In the New Testament, the importance of Pentecost is mainly described in Luke's two-volume work, the Gospel According to

Luke and the Acts of the Apostles. At Pentecost the apostles came to the *realization* that the Holy Spirit had been given them, or they at least experienced it as given in a new way. This experience might be compared with the experience of Jesus at his baptism and temptation, when he came to full consciousness of his person and destiny. Since Pentecost, Christians open to God's gift have been given the very Spirit of God, who had been revealed to them in the life, death, resurrection and ascension of Jesus. This spiritual reality, the very spirit that Jesus embodied, is now incarnated in dedicated Christian believers. Justin Martyr expressed it well and succinctly in these words: "Jesus became what we are in order that we might become what he is."

Mark's Gospel does not speak of the Pentecost event. After careful consideration of all of the evidence, I am convinced that we do not have the final pages of Mark's Gospel. Even if we did, however, I doubt if Mark would have described Pentecost in detail. This was not his purpose. His goal was to preserve the historical facts of Jesus' life. He probably wrote his work living in a resurrection-ascension-Spirit-filled time. He was so much a part of it that in his hurried, almost breathless presentation he did not reflect on all that had been given him and those to whom he ministered.

Matthew writes only a little about the giving of the Holy Spirit. That he knew of the action of the Spirit is clear when he quotes Jesus' telling his followers that when they were arrested they need not worry about what they should say, because "it will be the Spirit of your Father speaking in you" (10:20). And in the concluding scene of Matthew's Gospel, Jesus gathers his disciples around him and passes his authority on to them, telling them to baptize "in the name of the Father and the Son and the Holy Spirit, and to teach them to observe all that I commanded you" (28:20). Nonetheless, Matthew's interest was not so much in presenting the life of the Church in the apostolic age as in providing a new law and teaching and in preserving that tradition for future generations.

The Gospel According to John likewise ends with the actual ministry of Jesus of Nazareth. However, that gospel places great emphasis on the Paraclete, who cannot come until Jesus leaves and who will be the defender of the persecuted, the empowerer, the giver of wisdom and new life. In John 20:19ff, Jesus appears to the disciples, greets them, shows them his hands and feet, and then tells them: "As the Father has sent me, so I send you." Then he breathes on them and says, "Receive the Holy Spirit," and he goes on to give them authority to forgive or to retain human sins. John's tradition is certainly parallel to that of Luke. But John's purpose was to record the saving life-death-resurrection of Jesus rather than to record the effect of the gift of the Holy Spirit upon Jesus' followers.[3]

Luke had two purposes in writing. First, he provided a connected narrative about the events occurring around Jesus of Nazareth. Then he gave a history of what happened in the life of the Church as the Holy Spirit was poured out on Jesus' followers. Luke's second work, the Acts of the Apostles, demonstrates the continued presence and power of Jesus' Spirit in the life of the Church. Acts begins with a description of the ascension; it then goes on to tell of a powerful experience in which the disciples are filled with something they had not known before. The first action of Peter after receiving this gift is to preach with such persuasion that many are converted. The next recorded activity of the apostles is the healing of the lame man at the Beautiful Gate of the temple by Peter and John. It is clear from these descriptions that Jesus' power had passed on to the apostles. The Church continued to grow, and Stephen manifested the same Holy Spirit. As the leaders were about to stone Stephen, the Holy Spirit revealed to him Jesus standing at God's right hand. Then the risen and still present Jesus of Nazareth came to Paul and converted him. Paul was filled with the Holy Spirit and became one of the most important leaders of the nascent Church.

Paul's letters describe the action of the Holy Spirit, which provided the presence and power of the risen Jesus, in terms quite similar to those frequently used by Luke in Acts. Luke's second volume might be called a history of the Holy Spirit, and in several places Paul similarly describes the various powers or gifts of the Holy Spirit. The Christ-life was growing continually as more and more people became Christians and were filled with the Holy Spirit; the fire that was lit on Pentecost was consuming more and more of the world.

Luke described the original experience of fire in these words: "On the day of Pentecost all of them were together in one place, the disciples, the women who had been close to Jesus and others. Suddenly from heaven came the sound of powerful wind; this wind filled the entire house where they were sitting. And there appeared to them tongues like flames of fire that rested upon each of those there. And they were filled with the Holy Spirit and began to speak in other tongues that the Spirit gave them the power to speak" (Acts 2:1-4). It is much easier to make sense of this experience when we realize that modern men and women testify to similar experiences that have remade their lives. Here is the statement of a very normal person known to me who had such an experience in a prayer group in a church:

> I was kneeling as four others prayed for me. They put their hands on my head and on my shoulders . . . The prayer was simple—a request for a greater flow of Spirit within me. I was open and expectant. And then it happened! . . . It was like a baptism. I felt that I was going down, then coming up. Or, the feeling was like draining out, and refilling. It was all an inner thing—down and then up. As I "came up" I spoke in tongues and interpreted.
>
> Besides the tongues and the interpretation, my hands felt full, as if there was much to pass through them—and on out. I was filled with tremendous joy. Laughter came easily. It was tremendously exhilarating, and it was not easy to sleep that night! The next day was much the same. I felt different. I was different. . . . Passages of scripture I had read before and did not understand were opened in this

(the experience of tongues) and many other areas.[4]

The Meaning of Pentecost—Real Fellowship

This Christian experience of being filled with the Spirit of God is intimately linked to the loving, suffering, risen Jesus of Nazareth. And without the resurrection of Jesus, this experience makes no sense. Jesus' rising from the dead is more than a victory that occurred once; rather, resurrection came to fruition in the giving of the Holy Spirit. In a very real way, the Spirit imparted Jesus' victory to all people so that they could share in it.

The disciples in the Bible who received this spiritual reality underwent a profound experience—much like the religious experiences people still have today. First of all, they were washed free of many of the hindrances of their broken natures; they were forgiven. This opened up wells of life within them. And receiving the Spirit was not once for all; when they knew that such a reality was available, they could turn to it again and again and is regenerated bit by bit. The gift of the Holy Spirit enabled them to be open to participate in its life. The early Christians were given unbelievable courage and strength as they faced persecution, torture, and death. (Similarly, the prison doctor who watched theologian Dietrich Bonhoeffer die in the Nazi prison on April 9, 1945 reported that he had never seen anyone die so entirely submissive to the will of God.) The early Christians were given ghostly strength. In addition, the courage that Christians expressed as they were thrown to the lions transformed scornful opponents of Christianity into sympathetic onlookers and finally drew them into the fold. These early Christians even showed love to those who persecuted them, scorned them, and killed them.

The disciples were given new powers and abilities, described by Paul in several passages and described in individual instances in the historical narrative of Acts. The Spirit of Christ released or created abilities within them that they did not have before. The original band of Galilean peasants confronted the world of power and learning and eventually won this world over to their faith in the risen Jesus Christ. The spiritual domain of God and of the risen Jesus was opened to them in a new way; they were given revelations and divine guidance. Like Jesus, they had the power to heal the physically and mentally ill as well as the demon-possessed. Some of them spoke in ecstatic speech.

In Jesus of Nazareth love and power had met and mingled. In many of the early Christians the same love and power flowered. They claimed that it was the Spirit and presence of Jesus which gave them new life and power. A Zen Buddhist monk once remarked: "We think that there is something in Christianity, but we don't think that Christians know what it is." A friend of mine commented on this statement by remarking to me: "After twenty-five years in the Christian ministry, and fifteen of those spent in denominational service and ecumenical affairs, I would have to concede that the Buddhist monk has pretty big substantiation for his remark." I find myself wondering, of course, what the Zen Buddhist monk thought there might be in Christianity. My guess is that he made reference to a kind of spiritual power which sustained the early Christians under persecution.

This is the Spirit that is able to make all religious people one, the Spirit that flows through Chiara Lubich, the founder of the Focolare Movement. This experience of receiving the Holy Spirit can come to some people as it did to the apostles at Pentecost—as a rushing mighty wind and like tongues of fire that sear the heart. Such people have to remain open to that Spirit or they can become spiritually dead. To other people the Holy Spirit may come much more gradually, imperceptibly changing them until they are really quite different, incredibly caring and loving. It is important to realize that God treats each of us as individuals, giving us the Spirit in the way most meaningful, creative and congenial to us. The purpose of the Christian Church is to bring all different kinds of people into living relationship with each other and with the reality and Spirit of the risen Jesus. The goal of Christianity is to make silk purses out of sows' ears.

I do not know how the following poem came into my hands. I don't know the author. It is not great poetry, but it does give a sense of what many people have felt when they have been touched by the Spirit of the resurrected Jesus of Nazareth.

T'was battered, scarred, and the auctioneer
     thought it scarcely worth the while

To waste his time on the old violin,
   but he held it up with a smile.
"What am I bid, good people," he cried,
   "Who'll start the bidding for me?
One dollar? One dollar . . . now do I hear two?
   Two dollars . . . now who makes it three?

Three dollars once . . . three dollars twice, going
   for three . . ." But no!
From the room far back a greybearded man
   came forward and picked up the bow.
Then wiping the dust from the old violin
   and tightening up the strings
He played a melody, pure and sweet,
   as sweet as the angels sing.

The music ceased, and the auctioneer
   with a voice that was quiet and low
Said, "What now am I bid for the old violin?"
   As he held it aloft with its bow.
"One thousand?" said he. "Two thousand?
   and now two thousand and who makes it
     three?
Three thousand once, three thousand twice . . .
   and going and gone," said he.

The people cheered, but some of them cried,
   "We don't quite understand . . .
What changed its worth?" Swift came the
    reply,
   "The touch of a master's hand."

And many a man with life out of tune,
   all battered and torn with sin
Is auctioned cheap to a thoughtless crowd
   much like the old violin.

A mess of pottage, a glass of wine,
   a game, and he travels on
He is going once, he is going twice,
   he is going and almost gone.
But the Master comes and the foolish crowd
   never can quite understand
The worth of a soul, that change that was
      wrought
   by the touch of the Master's hand.

I heard a magnificent sermon by a black preacher. It was simply this poem, repeated with love and understanding. The preacher proclaimed the value of every human soul as powerfully as I have ever heard it done. Truly we are all one and all have infinite value as we are touched by God's hand.

People who have experienced the Spirit have often felt like useless earthen vessels filled with gold and precious stones, like broken cisterns made whole and filled with streams of living water, like old violins touched by the master's hand. Broken and tired humans, battered and used mortals, have become the dwelling place, the temple of Jesus' Spirit, and have gained incomparable worth.

In 1660, after being imprisoned in England for his religious beliefs, James Nayler was released and recon-

ciled with the Society of Friends. Shortly after that he
set out from London, intending to visit his wife and
children in Wakefield. On the way he was robbed,
beaten, and left bound in a field. Some members of the
Society of Friends found him; they brought him into
their home, where he died. About two hours before he
died, he spoke the following words, which were taken
down as he spoke them:

> There is a spirit which I feel that delights to
> do no evil, nor to revenge any wrong, but de-
> lights to endure all things, in hope to enjoy its
> own in the end. Its hope is to outlive all wrath
> and contention, and to weary out all exalta-
> tion and cruelty, or whatever is of a nature
> contrary to itself. It sees to the end of all
> temptations. As it bears no evil in itself, so it
> conceives none in thoughts to any other. If it
> be betrayed, it bears it, for its ground and
> spring is the mercies and forgiveness of God.
> Its crown is meekness, its life is everlasting
> love unfeigned; and takes its kingdom with
> entreaty and not with contention, and keeps
> it by lowliness of mind. In God alone it can re-
> joice, though none else regard it, or can own
> its life. It's conceived in sorrow, and brought
> forth without any to pity it, nor doth it mur-
> mur at grief and oppression. It never rejoiceth
> but through sufferings; for with the world's
> joy it is murdered. I found it alone, being for-
> saken. I have fellowship therein with them

who lived in dens and desolate places in the earth, who through death obtained this resurrection and eternal holy life.

These words could have been written to describe the suffering and victory of Jesus of Nazareth. The Spirit of which Nayler spoke was the Spirit of the risen Jesus; Nayler's life and death were an incarnation of Jesus and our God.

Such incarnational experiences happen in our day as well. An attractive and religious married woman recently shared an experience that she had as a child, an experience uncovered after work in spiritual direction. I had asked members of a group to share their most important religious experiences with me so I could share these with the group. I put the story in her words, though for obvious reasons I have changed details:

When I was nine years old, I was taken and very brutally attacked by three men for several hours. My whole inner being was begging to die in order to escape the physical pain I was experiencing. At one point I was in a semi-conscious state, and I could hear the men talking about how to dispose of my "dead" body. I could not speak or move to tell them I wasn't dead yet. I felt my body in the process of dying and was glad that I could finally escape the pain.

Then I became aware that I could choose whether I lived or died. When I realized I had a choice, I couldn't make up my mind. I had

strong feelings for both life and death. A voice
was telling me that time was running out and
I had to make a decision soon! Or it would be
too late—I would be irreversibly dead.

As I considered never seeing my "mommy"
and "daddy" again—their grief over my disap-
pearance—their sadness over not having me
with them—I chose to live.

After I made that choice I heard a voice telling me to move my body so the men would
know I was still alive. I could not move even a
muscle on my own. And then Jesus appeared
to me, standing by my right foot (I was on the
ground). He reached down and moved my
legs, and one of the men saw me move and
took compassion on me. The man wrapped
me in a blanket, took me to his dwelling,
cleaned me up and took me home.

I did not see Jesus' face. I just knew who he
was. I say he—but what I saw was a large, gentle white figure. There were no words—just an
atmosphere of deep, deep caring and a wave
of peace filled my body. All my pain and
bruises and cuts felt healed.

One of the central mysteries of the Christian faith is
the relation of the various persons of the Godhead and
particularly the relation of the risen Jesus and the Holy
Spirit. In this adult's story about her childhood experience, we find the Spirit prompting her to move her
body and to have the courage to live. This kind of expe-

rience is often associated with the action of the Holy Spirit. Then came the critical and unsought experience of the luminous, victorious Jesus standing by her and moving her leg. The dreamer experienced the resurrected Jesus Christ as a living, still available, present, saving reality. Experiences like this have occurred all through church history; they still occur today.[5]

The essential meaning of the experience of the Holy Spirit, the giving of the Paraclete (advocate, defender, redeemer), is the continued availability of the risen Jesus of Nazareth. This can be experienced as a Spirit within us, of which James Nayler spoke. The child in the dream also first experiences help in this way—as spirit. Or the specific, personal presence of Jesus, who conquered death and evil, can also be known and experienced. Such a meeting can be as transforming as it was for Mary Magdalene.

The resurrection has always been central in my religious belief. However, few modern theologians see its grandeur and centrality. I had my eyes opened by a German-Jewish theologian, Pinchas Lapide, who felt that Christians were not living up to their heritage. In his writing, this scholarly Jew writes profoundly about the resurrection of Jesus of Nazareth:

> All honest theology is a theology of catastrophe, a theology that receives its impulse from the misery and the nobility of our human nature;

From the fear of death, from the will to live, and from the great hope that not everything is at an end when death comes;

A hope that arises from an anticipation of that incomprehensible infinity and final reality which we call God;

A hope that cannot acquiesce in the thought that our existence begins with birth pangs and a whimper—only to end with a final rattle of agony;

A hope that tears, death, and mourning will not have the last word;

A hope that draws from its confidence "upward" the courage to look "ahead"; courage beyond dying to a life beyond the grave which deprives death of its sting in order to give our life a meaning which cannot perish or decay . . .

That is the quintessence of the biblical faith in the resurrection, both of Jews and Christians . . .

If one could gain an insight into the soul of today's surviving remnant of Israel in order to discover its understanding of itself, one would most likely draw the conclusion that Auschwitz and the founding of the State of Israel stand in the same spiritual relationship with each other as Good Friday and Easter Sunday do in the heart of believing Christians. The same abyss yawns between cross and the resurrection as between the mass Golgotha of the Hitler years and the national resurrection in the year 1948.

Without the resurrection of Jesus, after Golgotha, there would not have been any Christianity—just as Auschwitz without the successive new foundation of Israel could have meant the end of the Jewish people. For what Christian can ever know how much unfounded confidence and faith in the future is needed in order to bring Jewish children into the world since 1945? Thus, the cause of Jesus is basically the cause of Israel, both the doctrine and the suffering, the faith experience of God, the survival after martyrdom, and the eternal life for which we hope. Here I see the uniqueness of the basic meaning of that salvation event on Passover-Easter Sunday in Jerusalem.

A resurrection of our hope for life which Jews and Christians affirm in common.[6]

The next important question now presents itself. If Jesus' love and healing power are still available, how do we open ourselves to receive them?

Chapter 11

Our Response to Resurrection

When the feast was over and the bones of the fatted calf had been picked clean, was there any change in the prodigal son? He now realized the incredible love and forgiveness of his father, how much he was loved. Now it depended on him. Would he respond? Would he seek out his father's companionship and be molded by that love into the kind of person his father was? Would he seek out his brother and relate to him? Would he treat the servants in a new way? When he went out into the village and beyond would he be fair and kind to the just and the unjust? When he was discouraged would he return to his father for encouragement, enlightenment and love? The same questions could be asked of the elder brother. The same questions can be asked of us after we have really heard the resurrection story or after we have celebrated the feast of Easter. How can we continue to be vividly aware of Jesus' saving pres-

ence in us and in our midst? How can we continue to
share in his victory over evil and death? How do we respond to the divine drama so that its purpose can be
completed in us, so that Jesus' birth and life and death,
his resurrection and giving of himself in the Holy
Spirit, were not done for us in vain?

Love

At the core and center of Jesus' message and of his
life and death-resurrection is love divine, all loves excel-
ling. "Jesus became what we are in order that we might
become what he is." Jesus loved us human beings
enough to die for us because he expressed God's unfathomable love for us. We are called to live out love in
our daily circumstances as he did in his. In the parable
of the last judgment the righteous sheep are separated
from the goats on the basis of whether or not they ministered to the hungry, the lonely, the homeless, those in
prison. In John's Gospel, after Jesus washed his disciples' feet he gave them a new commandment: "Love
one another as I have loved you." Love is transitive. It is
not just my feeling of caring toward another; rather,
love is the caring concern and love another person experiences through my presence and actions. The resurrection of Jesus has not become fully effective and
transforming in my life until those around me experience love through me. One essential part of my response to resurrection is shaping my life according to
the pattern of Jesus' unconditional love for me. This

kind of love is not instinctual; it must be learned and takes unending patience and hard work.

Love means many things. It means social action, reaching out to the homeless, the broken, the discouraged, the confused, the poor, the suffering, the sick, the alcoholic, the mentally ill, the depressed, the hungry, those in prison, those addicted to drugs, and all who are suffering and are heavy-laden. But our social action can take on many different directions. It can mean to offer people a new world view so that they are not automatically cut off from an experience of God's love. Genuine social action seeks to release people from limitations, oppression and suffering. Each of us has our specific role and destiny to play in ministering to human misery. If we try to take on all the problems of the world we usually bog down and accomplish nothing. Each of us needs to ask: What is my task?

Love needs to be a way of life expressing itself on many different levels. We need to love ourselves as Jesus loves us; if we don't we may be unable to love others like ourselves. Nothing is more difficult for us humans to believe, nothing takes more prayer than to believe that God loves us unconditionally. Next we need to communicate that love to those closest to us. If we see only the suffering poor out in the world and do not love those hungry for love and attention within our own families, we are in danger of hypocrisy. We then need to see that our casual acquaintances, the people in the office or the club, need our love as well. Does our kindness and concern extend to the annoying clerk in the store, the one who cleans the room in the hotel, the dis-

courteous bus driver? Are we aware of the stranger in
our midst in the subway, at the cocktail party, at the
swimming pool? Do we reach out to them in a gesture
of friendship and concern? Do we recognize the enemy,
the one who can't stand us or the one who has wronged
us or the one who makes our hair bristle?

Love grows as we try to love our enemy. God in his
infinite concern for our growth will provide a new enemy when we have come to love the last one! We can
also show love by allowing others to help us when we
have need, accepting love graciously without constantly looking for the other's angle in giving caring. A
personal journal can be an indispensable aid in giving
us the opportunity to reflect on how we are loving and
how we are failing and on how to plan our lives so that
they may better express love. Growth in loving is a
never ending process.

Another way of loving is sharing with others the saving, transforming power of the ever-present risen Jesus
and his Spirit. This is a delicate matter. We need to be
sensitive to where people are. Badgering people before
we have listened to them is not love. Truly loving re-
quires being open to others and listening. Then as they
spill out their lostness, darkness, fear and confusion we
can offer them what we have been given by the resurrected Christ. Not to speak when there is need is as un-
loving as speaking before we have listened. We are
called to minister, not to badger and invade the lives of
others.

Christian and so-called Christian nations have not
always expressed loving concern for others in any

marked way; however the ideal of love is at least present as a goal. Where such an ideal is not present it cannot be realized. One reason that the early Church made such an impact on the Roman Empire was that the pagans looked at the Christians and said: "Look how they love one another." They hungered for that love and were drawn to the Christian fellowship in spite of the many risks involved.

Chapter 12

The Real Miracle

The real miracle of the rising of Jesus from the dead lies not in the fact that a dead body was raised from death and transformed into a radiant transcendence. The Creator who fashioned the infinite complexity and magnificence of the universe could certainly do that, but that is not what resurrection is about. The true miracle is what this resurrection reveals—the inhumanly loving God. In spite of the evil, ugliness, and pain of the world, at the center of reality abides the divine Lover keeping watch above us all. In spite of our failures, our rejection of love, our destructiveness, our pettiness, our violence, God loves us and continues to reach out to us. Jesus came into our world, lived, died, and rose again before we human beings even considered responding to God, simply to demonstrate that love for us, to manifest the truth that God is love.

The divine Lover is still knocking, waiting at the doorway of our souls to bring to fruition a life without bounds; this destiny is offered to us now in this world, and it continues on to fulfillment in the kingdom of God beyond this realm of time and space. This is the true miracle proclaimed by the resurrection.

Our final response is praise, like that of the Latin resurrection hymn. This hymn sums up the meaning of resurrection and the joy we are given by the victory of Jesus and God over the forces of evil and darkness.

> The strife is o'er, the battle done,
> The victory of life is won;
> The song of triumph has begun
> Allelluia! Alleluia! Alleluia! Alleluia!
>
> The powers of death have done their worst,
> But Christ their legions hath dispersed;
> Let shouts of holy joy outburst!
> Alleluia! Alleluia! Alleluia! Alleluia!
>
> The three sad days are quickly sped,
> He rises glorious from the dead;
> All Glory to our risen Head!
> Alleluia! Alleluia! Alleluia! Alleluia!
>
> He closed the yawning gate of hell,
> The bars from heaven's high portals fell;
> Let hymns of praise his triumphs tell!
> Alleluia! Alleluia! Alleluia! Alleluia!
>
> Lord! By the stripes which wounded thee,
> From death's dread sting thy servant's free!

That we may live and sing to thee!
Alleluia! Alleluia! Alleluia! Alleluia.[1]

Notes

Introduction

1. Reynolds Price, *Three Gospels* (New York: Scribner, 1996).
2. Translation by author.
3. Nella Braddy, *The Standard Book of British and American Verse* (North Stratford, NH: Ayer Co. Publ., Inc., 1972), pp. 611 ff.
4. In Greek, dark means what it does in English and also anything opposed to God.

Chapter 1

1. Dorothy Sayers' book *The Man Born to Be King* (London: Victor Gallancz Ltd., 1949) has been presented in many different editions. It is one of the most convincing and moving pictures of Jesus' life, death and resurrection. I would recommend it to everyone as devotional reading.

Chapter 2

1. In chapter 10 of my book, *The Drama of Christmas* (Louisville, KY: Westminster John Knox Press, 1994) I devote a chapter to these tentacles of divine brilliance that reach out to us.

2. Christian theology is written from this scientific point of view by John Polkinghorne in his 1994 Gifford Lectures, *Science and Christian Belief* (London: SPCK, 1994).

Chapter 3

1. G. Scott Sparrow, *I Am With You Always* (New York: Bantam Books, 1995).

Chpater 5

1. Only Cleopas is mentioned by name.
2. *The Comedy of Dante Alighieri*, Cantica III, Paradise; trans. by Dorothy Sayers and Barbara Reynolds (Baltimore: Penguin Books, Inc., 1962), p. 347.
3. This story is told by Arthur Gossip in his exposition of John's Gospel in George Arthur Buttrick, *The Interpreter's Bible* (Nashville, Tenn.: Abingdon Press, 1952), 8:793.

Chapter 6

1. This dialogue follows but changes Dorothy Sayers' account in *The Man Born to Be King*, pp. 334-35. I repeat that this presentation of the resurrection narrative is the most convincing attempt that I have seen to bring together the various appearances.
2. Henri Bergson, *The Two Sources of Morality and Religion* (Garden City, N.Y.: Doubleday and Company, 1935), p. 315.
3. *The Interpreter's Bible*, 8:418.

Chapter 7

1. John J. Brugaletta is Professor of English at California State University, Fullerton, California. This poem, "The Beast of Bethany," was published in *Plains Poetry Journal*, July 1983, pp. 28-31, and is used with the permission of both the

author and the journal. The author's title refers to the presence of death that surrounded Jesus and his disciples as they went up to Jerusalem.

Chapter 8

1. This meeting is described in the last chapter of John's Gospel and was evidently added before the Gospel was circulated but after the first twenty chapters had been completed. For those who wish a scholarly discussion of this story and the rest of the Fourth Gospel, there is none better than Raymond Brown's *Anchor Bible Commentary, The Gospel According to John XIII-XXI* (Garden City: Doubleday and Company, Inc., 1970). This work deals with the critical problems with good sense as well as with scholarship and interprets the religious dimensions of John's Gospel. I draw heavily upon this important work.

2. C. S. Lewis, *The Lion, the Witch and the Wardrobe* (Middlesex, England: Penguin Books, 1950), pp. 147-48.

Chapter 9

1. James Kirsch, *The Reluctant Prophet* (Los Angeles: Sherbourne Press, 1973), chap. 13, pp. 132ff.

2. *The Hymnal of the Episcopal Church in the USA* (Greenwich, Conn.: The Seabury Press, 1943), hymn no. 354.

Chapter 10

1. I have described the history of this movement and the experience of tongue speaking which has often been associated with it in my book *Tongue Speaking: The History and Meaning of Charismatic Experience* (New York: Crossroad, 1981). I have provided in this book numerous examples of regeneration associated with an experience of the Holy Spirit.

2. Paul describes the gifts of the Holy Spirit in 1 Corinthians 12:6ff as nine in number. I have described them as belonging to five categories: the gift of healing and miracles, the gift of

revelation in visions, dreams and communication, the gift of discerning spirits (the ability to distinguish good spiritual influences from evil), the gift of extrasensory knowing, and finally the gift of proclamation (prophecy, tongues and the interpretation of tongues). In addition there is the important gift of being able to love in the Christian sense and the gift of knowing and experiencing those who are a part of the communion of saints in heaven.

3. Raymond Brown provides a careful analysis of this passage in his commentary. In Appendix V: The Paraclete, in *The Gospel According to John XIII-XXI*, pp. 135-43, he also provides a study of the meaning of this word in John.

4. Morton Kelsey, *Tongue Speaking*, pp. 134-35.

5. G. Scott Sparrow has given evidence for this in his recent book, *I Am with You Always* (New York: Bantam Books, 1995).

6. Pinchas Lapide, *The Resurrection of Jesus* (Minneapolis: Augsburg, 1983), pp. 148-49.

Chapter 12

1. *The Hymnal of the Episcopal Church in the USA*, hymn no. 91, ancient Latin translated by Francis Potts in the middle of the nineteenth century.

Also available from New City Press

SET YOUR HEARTS ON THE GREATEST GIFT
Living the Art of Christian Love
by Morton Kelsey,

"A wise and compassionate book from Morton Kelsey, who distills a lifetime's learning and teaching about love in these pages. Poet, teacher, and psychologist, Kelsey uses his own rich experience to explain how we can grow in Christian love."

Spirit & Life

"This rich and full book is a cry of joy and hope to the church and to each one of us about what is the essence of the essence. Read it if you want to be reinspired by the core values of the Christian faith. Give it to anyone who wonders what Christianity is really about. Morton condenses a lifetime of wisdom and experience into this very readable compendium on love. Would that every Christian would read it. What a great selection for group study as well as personal reflection!"

Book Nook

"Kelsey writes movingly about his own slow learnings in the art of love during his son's battle with death. The best section of the book revolves around his own nighttime talks with God."

Values & Visions Magazine

ISBN 1-56548-043-0
paperback, 53/8 x 81/2, 216 pp., $10.95

To order phone 1- 800 - 462-5980

And . . .

SPIRITUAL LIVING IN A MATERIAL WORLD
A Practical Guide
by Morton Kelsey

"Morton Kelsey's book is clear, practical, helpful, encouraging, and solid. Those who are searching or beginning the exciting adventure into God will find effective tools for spirit-filled living. Those who are already on the way will be reminded, supported, and encouraged."

Sister Rita Ann Houlihan
Sisters of the Cenacle

ISBN 1-56548-105-4
paperback, 51/8 x 8, 96 pp., $6.95

WHAT IS HEAVEN LIKE?
The Kingdom as Seen in the Beatitudes
by Morton Kelsey

Is there an afterlife? What is it like? Is there anyway to know?

"This is a book at once kind and gentle, wonderful and exciting, informative and practicle. Here you will find many insights into this life and the next by a gifted writer."

Mitch Finley
Author

ISBN 1-56548-091-0
paperback, 51/8 x 8, 96 pp., $6.95

To order phone 1- 800 - 462-5980